O

in

Paralegal Careers

OPPORTUNITIES

in

Paralegal Careers

REVISED EDITION

ALICE FINS

McGraw·Hill

New York   Chicago   San Francisco   Lisbon   London   Madrid   Mexico City
Milan   New Delhi   San Juan   Seoul   Singapore   Sydney   Toronto

The *McGraw·Hill* Companies

Library of Congress Cataloging-in-Publication Data

Fins, Alice.
Opportunities in paralegal careers / Alice Fins.— Rev. ed.
p.   cm.
ISBN 0-07-143844-0
1. Legal assistants—Vocational guidance—United States.   2. Legal assistants—
United States.   I. Title.

KF320.L4F56   2005
340'.023'73—dc22   2004025054

1 2 3 4 5 6 7 8 9 0   DOC/DOC   0 9 8 7 6 5

ISBN 0-07-143844-0

Interior design by Rattray Design

McGraw-Hill books are available at special quantity discounts to use as premiums and sales promotions, or for use in corporate training programs. For more information, please write to the Director of Special Sales, Professional Publishing, McGraw-Hill, Two Penn Plaza, New York, NY 10121-2298. Or contact your local bookstore.

This book is printed on acid-free paper.

CONTENTS

9. Related Careers in the Courts 103

Court administrators. Other professional positions.
Counselors and social workers. Clerical positions.
Clerks of the court. Court reporters. Security
officials. Parajudges.

Foreword

THE PARALEGAL PROFESSION is interesting, challenging, and exciting. It is considered by many to be their chosen profession and not just a stepping-stone to law school.

Where once a paralegal position was attained primarily through experience and promotion within the law firm, today there is a growing interest in and need for higher education, and there is a wide variety of educational facilities from which to choose. A paralegal may achieve a paralegal certificate or an associate, a bachelor's, and even a master's degree in paralegal studies. Opportunities to specialize in certain areas of law are also growing.

It is imperative that those considering the paralegal profession be aware of the educational and/or experience requirements they will need to meet, depending upon the jurisdiction and the employment environment. The paralegal profession, while being one of the fastest growing in the nation, is still, for the most part, self directed. There are several paralegal associations, all of which have different definitions of *paralegal*. Likewise, many states are beginning to define standards (education and/or experience levels) as well as for whom a paralegal can provide services. Persons interested in becoming a paralegal should closely check the region in which they will likely seek employment to find if there are any specific requirements or criteria for paralegals, since there is no standardization.

Private law firms, corporations, financial institutions, insurance companies, government agencies, the courts, and numerous others have found that paralegals provide a cost-effective means of providing services to their clients. Additionally, paralegals with specialized skills, knowledge, and expertise are extremely advantageous in working with complex matters.

For instance, a paralegal with a medical background may be a wonderful asset to an insurance company or to a private law firm specializing in personal injury or medical malpractice. Likewise, a paralegal with financial or real estate experience may find a niche in both private firms and financial institutions for trust administration or real estate transactions. Most recently, knowledge of computer technology is a key component in a paralegal's education as well as in his or her career advancement. Certifications in specialized legal software are becoming more common. At the very least, a paralegal needs to be familiar with software for calendar, time keeping, word processing, and presentations. Also helpful is knowledge of the creation of databases and spreadsheets to manage data and documents. The area of electronic discovery is in its infancy and is rapidly changing. Those paralegals who are willing to keep abreast of newly developed rules, regulations, and statutes that govern electronic discovery will be on the ground floor of this emerging area of law and its implementation.

Paralegals will also learn that there is a variety of continuing education available once they have become paralegals. While continuing education is not currently required in jurisdictions other than

California, it is always a good idea to keep abreast of any new developments in the law, technology, and local rules on which the paralegal will rely. The law, like the paralegal profession, is constantly evolving and changing. This adds to the challenge and keeps us on top of our game. There are also certification tests that a paralegal may wish to take to challenge his or her skills and knowledge.

This book provides a wonderful overview of the profession in general, the types of employment opportunities available, and valuable insights into potential career paths.

Dianna L. Smiley, RP
President
National Federation of Paralegal Associations

1

SIMILAR JOBS, DIVERSE TITLES

THE TERM *PARALEGAL* is a common one, but it is only one of many titles used to describe a variety of similar jobs. Paralegals—and others with any number of job titles—perform a wide variety of functions ranging from clerical to administrative work.

Just what a paralegal job is called may reflect the scope and setting of the work. When examining classified advertisements for paralegal jobs, looking under the heading "paralegal" may not be sufficient. Instead, start with the "A" listings under "assistant" or "aide" and work your way through at least the "T's" and "title clerk." As William P. Statsky notes in *The Education of Legal Paraprofessionals*: "The field is already suffering from an overdose of terminology: lay practitioner, sublegals and paralegals, legal paraprofessionals, legal executive, legal service assistant, ombudsperson, lay advocate, legal nurse, legal technician, legal counselor, lay counselor, legal assistant, legal administrative technician, lay assistant, lay representative and so forth."

And still the possibilities go on. Other titles for paralegals include: professional legal secretary, community worker, community aide, lay associate, subprofessional assistant, managing clerk, nonlawyer assistant, mediator, consumer specialist, welfare advocate, block worker, legal aide, health advocate, consumer claims adjuster, legal computer specialist, referral agent, case finder, office assistant, probate assistant, litigation assistant, title clerk, business assistant, forum judge, and parajudge.

In each setting where paralegals are employed, separate terminology may be used with important distinctions; however, employers do not always agree on these distinctions. Before considering any job, find out what duties, responsibilities, and restrictions come with the title. For the purposes of this book, the most common titles you will see are paralegal or legal assistant.

Employers and Job Specialties

Paralegals and legal assistants hold about two hundred thousand jobs, according to the U.S. Department of Labor. About 70 percent are employed by private law firms. Most of the others work for corporate legal departments or government agencies. The U.S. Department of Justice is the largest federal employer of paralegals. The Social Security Administration and Department of Treasury are also major employers, as are state and municipal governments. A small number of paralegals own their own businesses and work as freelance legal assistants, contracting their services to attorneys or corporate legal departments.

While working for these and other employers, paralegals are involved in a number of different areas of the law. They deal with litigation, labor law, employee benefits, personal injury, corporate law, criminal law, intellectual property, bankruptcy, immigration, family law, and real estate, among other areas. Within specialties, paralegals may deal with specific areas of focus. For example, paralegals specializing in criminal law might work exclusively in helping process arrest documents.

Job duties of paralegals may vary widely in different types of organizations. Paralegals employed in corporations may help prepare and file annual financial reports, maintain corporate minute books and record resolutions, or prepare forms to secure loans for the corporation. They may also assist attorneys with employee contracts, shareholder agreements, stock-option plans, and employee benefit plans.

Those employed in government agencies or nonprofit organizations perform duties such as conducting research for attorneys, analyzing legal material for internal use, maintaining reference files, and collecting and analyzing evidence for agency hearings. They may also prepare information about laws, regulations, and agency policy for general use by the agency and the public.

Some paralegals are employed in community legal-service projects. They help the poor, the elderly, or others who need legal assistance. Typical duties include filing forms, conducting research, preparing documents, and where the laws allow, representing clients at administrative hearings.

Two Basic Work Categories

The work done by paralegals may be divided into two basic categories. One is the area of administrative support performed by an administrative assistant. The other category is legal assistance performed by a legal specialist—usually a paralegal.

The administrative assistant may perform such tasks as office and personnel management, typing, accounting, timekeeping, billing, filing, maintaining a library, and routine investigating.

The legal specialist, or paralegal, may perform skilled tasks in substantive areas of law such as divorce, probate, corporation practice, and real estate.

Paralegals generally work under the direct supervision of lawyers. Although the lawyers assume responsibility for the legal work, they often delegate many of the tasks they perform to paralegals.

Paralegals usually do the background work for lawyers in preparing cases for trial. In general, paralegals:

1. Investigate the facts of cases, ensuring that all relevant information is uncovered
2. Conduct legal research to identify the appropriate laws, judicial decisions, legal articles, and other materials that may be relevant to assigned cases
3. Organize and analyze all the information and prepare written reports for attorneys to use in determining how cases should be handled
4. Prepare the legal arguments, draft pleadings and motions to be filed with the court, obtain affidavits, and assist the attorneys during the trials
5. Keep files of all documents and correspondence important to cases

Many legal specialists develop their expertise by first gaining experience in performing administrative tasks. The route from legal secretary to paralegal is one that is frequently taken.

Employers, especially small private firms, often hire paralegals and expect them to perform much of the time as administrative assistants.

Legal Assistants and Legal Advocates

Another distinction is often made between legal assistants and legal advocates. A legal assistant helps a lawyer in the practice of law or in the production of a legal service. The legal advocate is a person who acts in a representative or advice-giving capacity. The legal advocate is not necessarily supervised by a lawyer. The legal advocate generally works in nonlawyer-dominated institutions, often in the public sector such as in prisons, labor unions, community organizations, and administrative agencies. The legal advocate may have only occasional contact with the lawyer.

Generally, the legal assistant relies mostly on reading and writing skills. By contrast, the legal advocate may plead, intercede, or speak for another person; argue for a proposal; and give advice. The advocate also must understand how groups and institutions function. Based on this knowledge, advocates are often able to persuade institutions to be responsive to the needs of their clients.

The legal advocate is not confined to advocacy of causes and claims on behalf of individuals and groups. Legal advocates also are employed by government agencies, such as the Federal Trade Commission, as research analysts or ombudspersons. Duties of legal advocates may include recording complaints or participating in investigations to determine whether the complaints contain a cause of action that is within the agency's jurisdiction.

Legal advocates may handle other law enforcement assistance activity that centers on securing compliance with the law and regulations that their agency is charged with enforcing. They may assist in adjudication of disputes within the agency's authority. They may participate in decisions on whether to accord agency benefits to those who claim eligibility.

The growth of administrative agencies has supplied great impetus to the development of legal advocacy. In most cases, nonlawyers may represent people before administrative agencies on both federal and state levels.

Lay-legal advocates are allowed a wider range of decision-making roles than legal specialists. Legal advocates use fewer legal forms or law office manuals. They also are more free to select courses of action, determine strategies, and recommend outcomes.

In a typical lawsuit, the work involved includes skilled tasks such as interviewing the client, researching points of law, drafting pleadings, and arguing the case before a judicial body. The legal assistant might perform some of the research and draft the pleadings; the advocate might interview the client and argue the case. However, the advocate also may do some research and prepare pleadings, or the assistant may get information directly from the client before drawing up a petition. Sometimes legal assistants not only file the papers with the clerk of the court, but also respond to the calling of the roll. Appearance in court is prohibited to paralegals under some state laws.

Another illustration of an individual who does the work of both advocate and legal assistant is the jailhouse writer. This legal paraprofessional (although incarcerated) solicits and provides a wide range of legal services. This paralegal's services may include legal researching, brief and writ writing, and giving legal advice.

2

PARALEGALS PAST AND PRESENT

As it exists today, the legal system of the United States is extremely formal and highly structured. But it has not always been that way. During colonial times, many people had a distrust of the formal procedures used by lawyers. They either represented themselves in disputes or had persons who were not legally trained speak for their interests.

Beginnings of the Legal Profession

In the early days of the United States, almost anyone could become a lawyer or judge without meeting rigorous training requirements. In fact, the first judges in the United States were not lawyers. Indiana, like many other states, permitted any morally upright voter to practice law in its courts. Even today, many judicial positions are open to nonlawyers.

In the past, lawyers often got their training by reading the law. Abraham Lincoln became a lawyer in this way. Clarence Darrow, another famous lawyer, received no formal legal training. Simply reading about the law and then taking a bar examination is still permitted in a few states, but with many strings attached. Generally the practice of law requires graduation from an American Bar Association–approved law school and successful completion of a state bar examination.

In early times, before typewriters or word processors, lawyers needed apprentices—people who could write clearly—to prepare copies of documents in longhand. With the rise of industrialization in the nineteenth century came specialization in law practice, and an increased concern for organization and efficiency.

Before that time, most lawyers usually had been solo practitioners who did everything themselves. When this tendency began to change, there was much resistance from older lawyers, who believed that lawyers should not delegate any duties to non-lawyers. To do so, the older lawyers argued, would corrupt the practice of law. Remnants of this attitude are still encountered today, but now all lawyers recognize the need for a clerical and secretarial staff. Most lawyers also welcome other nonlegal staff, including paralegals.

The Advent of Bar Associations

Experts on the law generally consider the modern legal period to have begun in 1870 with the establishment of the Association of the Bar of New York City. Many bar associations were formed in subsequent decades at state and local levels. Among their purposes were disciplining lawyers and protecting attorneys from the encroachment of nonlawyers. From 1776 to 1829, seventeen states passed laws restricting entrance into the legal profession.

Between 1830 and 1870, ironically, practically all the states removed these restrictions. In 1850, the Michigan constitutional convention declared, "Every person at the age of twenty-one years, of good moral character, shall have the right to practice in any court in this state."

One reason for removing these restrictions was the mood of the times. In an era when people tended to fend for themselves, many were suspicious that specialized education and organized occupations would restrict people's natural rights.

Another factor may have been that lawyers were considered an elite group. To some, they represented wealthy and landed interest or creditors who could ruin individual citizens. While some people still view lawyers in this way, their elitist image has diminished, at least to some extent, with the growth of poverty law firms and legal services that help the disadvantaged gain access to their legal rights.

With the advent of legal clinics and prepaid legal insurance, legal services have become more available to the middle class and those of limited means. These legal options necessitate the operation of law offices on an affordable and efficient basis and are predicated on the use of paralegals. However, the use of paralegals did not occur without some struggles.

Origins of the Paralegal Profession

As the importance of the legal profession began to grow, there emerged a need for staff assistance. At the same time, the rise of administrative agencies created increasing demands for personnel to fill specialized roles.

Needs of Private Law Offices

At the end of the nineteenth century, lawyers began to hire typists, librarians, investigators, and other staff personnel. As firms grew larger, supervisory roles were created, such as head or chief secretary and finance manager. These lay assistants provided help in addition to the services rendered by specialists such as accountants, tax and investment specialists, and, in some cases, research assistants.

Along with the growth of large law firms came the need for experts in office management. Generally, the office manager has a background in personnel and management and has some familiarity with the law. The office manager usually reports to the senior partner of the law firm. Often a person may attain this position by rising through the ranks—perhaps working up from secretary to head secretary, to administrative assistant, and then to office manager. In other cases, a person may become an office manager because of professional management training.

Growth of Administrative Agencies

Concurrent with the growth of the private law office was the growth of administrative agencies, primarily parts of the executive branch of government. Each agency established its own rules and procedures, which were often confusing to the ordinary citizen. To help people wade through these bureaucracies and get needed help or information, the position of legal advocate was developed. The legal advocate (see also Chapter 1) is a nonlawyer who serves as a specialist in agency procedures and helps citizens gain access to their government and their rights.

Congress and state legislatures, in spite of some bar opposition, permit laypersons to represent clients before administrative agencies. A milestone in this area was the Administrative Procedure Act of 1946. It authorizes federal agencies to permit laypersons to practice before them. Because of this act, thousands of citizens have had lay representation for problems involving administrative agency determinations.

Many politicians have recognized the need for citizen access and have hired people to help their constituents process their claims, such as obtaining veteran's benefits. Trade unions also employ agency experts or legal advocates to help their members, especially during strikes, when union members must be able to obtain benefits available from governmental agencies. For example, in the 1950s, the United Auto Workers of America (UAW) provided a union counselor to help striking employees obtain unemployment compensation and other benefits. The UAW and other unions still train individuals to serve in this capacity. Other labor organizations, such as the AFL-CIO, provide their members with such services through a union or rehabilitation counselor. They also offer their members group legal services.

When the federal government established the Office of Economic Opportunity in 1964 (later replaced by the Office of Community Services), legal services became available to the poor through a national network of nonprofit corporations. Until this time, disadvantaged citizens had to rely on gratuitous help from the organized bar or from poorly financed legal aid societies, or go unrepresented. The OEO, by employing paralegals, was able to make legal services affordable. The bulk of legal services for the poor has involved administrative law cases, such as obtaining welfare benefits or helping people get unemployment compensation.

The OEO experience with paralegals attracted the attention of lawyers in private practice. They began to realize the potential of the paralegal to increase the efficiency of their legal practice methods and thus increase their incomes.

Interest of the Organized Bar in Paralegals

The organized bar has a strong interest in paralegals. As early as 1968, the American Bar Association formed a Special Committee on Lay Assistants. Because of the connotations of this name, the committee changed its name to Standing Committee on Legal Assistants. This group has been active in promoting the use of paralegals and examining the training they receive.

Paralegal Organizations

In the 1970s, paralegals began to organize. Several groups with differing aims and philosophies arose. They include state and local paralegal associations that represent their members' interests through job banks, salary surveys, and other professional services, including professional seminars on the law and paralegal training.

In 1974, the National Federation of Paralegal Associations was formed, and a number of others have been formed over the past few decades, including the American Association for Paralegal Education, the Canadian Association of Paralegals, the Legal Assistant Management Association, the National Association of Legal Assistants, and the National Federation of Paralegal Associations (see Appendix A). See Appendix B for a selected list of legal periodicals.

Outlook for Paralegals

The U.S. Department of Labor projects that the number of jobs for paralegals and legal assistants will grow faster than the average for all occupations through 2012. This growth should take place for several reasons.

One factor is the trend of law firms and other employers with legal staffs to hire more paralegals to lower costs. Another factor is the desire of providers to expand the availability and efficiency of legal services. While the majority of job openings will be new jobs created by employment growth, other job openings will occur as currently employed paralegals retire, change careers, or otherwise leave the field. Demand for paralegals should also grow as an expanding and aging population requires legal services. Areas of special interest may include legal issues related to health care, intellectual property, international commence, senior citizens' needs, and the environment. The growth of prepaid legal plans also should contribute to the demand for legal services.

A similar growth pattern has emerged in Canada. There are now more than thirty thousand paralegals, legal assistants, and law clerks working across Canada, according to statistics published by Humber College. Prior to 1990 this figure stood at fewer than twenty thousand. Demand is expected to grow for Canadian positions such as small claims court agent, provincial offences prosecutor, legal researcher, investigator, court monitor, search/investigator of public records, and paralegal firm manager.

Notwithstanding all this growth in Canada and the United States, it is also important to realize that although more job openings may occur, competition will still be a consideration for job applicants. As training programs continue to produce trained graduates seeking employment, it will be important for any applicant to be well prepared.

It is expected that private law firms will continue to be the largest employers of paralegals. At the same time, opportunities will expand in other organizations such as banks, insurance companies, corporate legal departments, and real estate firms. As corporations look for ways to reduce expenses of operating, paralegal employment will continue to increase, and the range of tasks assigned to paralegals should expand.

Job growth can also be expected in government agencies and nonprofit organizations. For example, community legal-service programs, which provide assistance to the poor, elderly, minorities, and middle-income families, will be a source of additional jobs. The same will be true of various government agencies, consumer organizations, and the court system.

Of course, growth in paralegal jobs can be affected at any given time by the state of the economy. During economic downturns, demand may decline for some legal services, such as planning estates, drafting wills, and handling real estate transactions. When business is weak, corporations may be less inclined to initiate certain types of litigation or conduct other transactions involving legal work. As a result, paralegals employed in offices that are substantially affected by an economic downturn may be laid off or have their work hours reduced. Concurrently, others legal matters may actually see growth during the same period, due to bankruptcies, foreclosures, and divorces. Because they perform legal services at lower costs than attorneys, paralegals may fare better than many other workers in times of challenging economic change.

Use of Electronic Technologies

Looking to the future, the use of electronic technologies for legal research, document production, communications, and others purposes will be a major part of the paralegal's role. In recent years, paralegals have become increasingly responsible for computerized research, electronic document control, computer programs for law office management, and other technological aspects of the practice of law. In the process, computer use and technical knowledge have become essential to paralegal work, and this trend is almost certain to continue. This will include using computer software packages and the Internet to search legal literature, and using computer databases to retrieve, organize, and index law-related materials. It will also include expanded use of imaging software to scan documents directly into databases, computerized billing programs to help track hours billed to clients, and other functions. Job applicants and working paralegals with strong computer skills will definitely have an advantage in finding new positions or succeeding on the job.

3

EDUCATIONAL PREPARATION

DIFFERENT TYPES OF training and experience can lead to employment in paralegal jobs. Some types of training are more suitable for paralegals in private law offices; a different type of background or training may be needed for paralegals in community service.

It is a good idea to spend some time on the phone or to visit potential employers before investing time and money in any training program. You might want to compare several programs before enrolling at any given school. For a list of paralegal training programs, see Appendix C.

In some cases, you may not need specialized training. Some offices and agencies have their own training programs. They may, however, require prior paralegal preparation. To find out what route of training is best for you, contact potential employers and ask about their paralegal employment requirements.

On-the-Job Training

Some employers of paralegals simply want to employ a bright individual whom they can train. In some cases, employers are willing to pay for continuing education courses for their paralegals. Certain bar associations, such as the Illinois State Bar Association, offer courses for paralegals and require that an attorney attend along with the paralegal.

Formal Training Programs

Some students proceed directly from high school to collegiate programs in paralegal studies. Others take a less direct path, bridging from another career area. In fact, the paralegal field may be especially well suited to the needs of those seeking a second career.

The training route you choose depends on your background and experience. A woman who is reentering the labor market after raising a family, for example, may find that the maturity and organizational skills she gained as a homemaker are useful to a private lawyer specializing in real estate or probate.

Before selecting a training program, find out what type of placement service is available. Also, request the names of some recent graduates, so you may talk with them and find out if they thought their training was useful and whether they were able to get jobs.

Many schools and training institutions promise placement assistance. This assistance may run the gamut from offering a seminar in résumé writing to matching candidates with employers or transmitting application materials for students or graduates. On the other hand, some paralegals are left to their own resources in finding employment.

With both a growing number of attorneys and an increasing number of paralegals, competition is becoming quite stiff. If you decide on a formal training program, be sure it is one that will help you find a job once your training is completed.

According to the U.S. Department of Labor, formal paralegal training programs are offered by approximately six hundred colleges and universities, law schools, and proprietary schools. About 250 of these programs are approved by the American Bar Association (ABA). This approval is not a requirement for a program to be valid, and many schools have not applied for it. At the same time, some employers may give preference to graduates of an ABA-approved program in making decisions regarding hiring or promotion.

What does it take to get admitted to a paralegal program? Some schools require only a high school diploma. Others expect completion of specified college courses or a bachelor's degree, or a combination of education and related work experience. For some programs, applicants must complete standardized tests and take part in personal interviews.

Because entry into the paralegal field is open to a wide range of individuals with diverse educational backgrounds and work experiences, the length of training and admission requirements vary considerably from one institution to another.

The American Bar Association Standing Committee of Legal Assistants has noted: "Candidates' personal qualifications for admission into a legal assistant program are very important. Applicants must be able to write clearly, communicate effectively, and possess a high degree of motivation and analytical reasoning capability. They should also be responsible, mature individuals who are sincerely interested in pursuing a career as a legal assistant."

Associate Degree Programs

A common path to a paralegal career is obtaining a two-year associate of arts or associate of science degree. Two-year associate degree programs are offered by comprehensive community colleges and some four-year colleges and universities Although many community and technical colleges have an open-door admissions policy, many of the legal assistant education programs offered in them have developed selective admission criteria. This means that although admission to the college itself is virtually guaranteed, the same may not be true of programs in legal assisting or related areas.

Most paralegal training programs require a considerable amount of study and numerous assignments outside of class. To ensure that only qualified persons enter these programs, some schools employ screening devices such as test scores on college-level entrance examinations, special verbal aptitude tests, samples of writing ability, letters of recommendation, and personal interviews.

The curriculum in an associate degree program usually consists of a combination of general education courses and law-related and legal specialty courses. In most cases, the courses required in the legal specialty portion of the program have been designed and selected by educational administrators in consultation with members of the legal community. Trends, needs, and changes in the local legal community will therefore affect course requirements in legal specialty areas.

Ordinarily, an associate degree program provides students with the skills needed to perform as generalists. This means that students will receive instruction in several different legal specialty areas. Some of the legal specialty classes commonly required or offered as electives are legal research and writing, business law, introduction to paralegalism, law-office management, real estate, corporations, litigation, estate planning and administration, domestic relations, income tax and accounting, criminal law, insurance, and torts.

Bachelor's Degree Programs

Some colleges and universities offer four-year bachelor of arts or bachelor of science programs with a major or minor in legal assistant studies. Curriculum requirements include general education, business, and law-related and legal specialty courses.

The typical four-year program takes the approach of both a generalist and specialist to legal specialty topics. The generalist approach is similar to the curriculum offerings in an associate-degree program. Most often the courses taken during the last two years of the program are of a more intensive nature and allow the student to concentrate on one or more areas of legal specialization. This helps the student develop expertise in those selected areas. In addition, some four-year programs offer (and may require) several courses pertaining to the management and administration of law offices.

Most four-year programs provide students with both a sound liberal arts education and legal specialty training in several areas. Ideally, such preparation enables graduates to choose from a wide number of employment opportunities in various legally related occupations as well as in private law firms.

Certificate Programs

Nondegree certificate programs are offered by a number of universities, colleges, business schools, and proprietary schools. A certificate program offers only legal specialty training. Because the general education component is not included in their curricula, some programs require completion of one to two years of college, or more, prior to admission. Others follow a streamlined approach designed as an alternative to collegiate studies.

Some certificate programs are restricted to college graduates whose academic record displays a high level of achievement. Classes may be offered full-time during the day or on a part-time evening basis. Typically, the duration of the program ranges from three to twenty-four months. Students usually have the option of enrolling in one legal specialty concentration or in a general practice curriculum that may include some specialty training. Legal specialty concentrations that are frequently offered include real estate, litigation, estate planning and administration, corporations, and employee benefits.

Curriculum

Most paralegal programs cover the following subjects in addition to requiring general education either as part of the program or before it. The coverage of each subject varies according to the structure and length of the program:

- Introductory paralegal course
- Litigation or civil procedure
- Legal research and writing
- Legal ethics
- Specialized courses in one or more areas including real property/real estate transactions; wills, trusts, and estate planning/probate; family law; and business and corporate law and practice

Other subjects frequently offered include taxation, bankruptcy, contracts, commercial law, family law, and torts. Many schools also have one or more classes covering computer applications for legal assistants.

A Look at Some Paralegal Programs

In considering educational options, it can be helpful to review program requirements and course offerings. Here is a look at several paralegal programs offered by colleges and universities.

St. Petersburg Junior College

As previously noted, many two-year colleges (which may be known as community, junior, or technical colleges) offer associate degree programs in legal assisting or related areas. Normally, such programs can be completed in two academic years.

Some programs are offered during the evening, requiring a longer period to complete but having the advantage of being fully accessible to working students. For example, most students enrolling in the legal assisting program offered by St. Petersburg Junior College in Florida take ten or eleven semesters to fulfill degree requirements, completing two or three classes per semester.

Students who complete this program learn to:

- Demonstrate a basic understanding of legal concepts and terminology
- Understand and explain the organization and jurisdiction of federal and state court systems
- Understand and explain the organization and functions of the law firm and its personnel
- Perform basic legal research and writing

- Provide a general understanding of recognized ethical standards and rules of professional responsibility
- Demonstrate the ability to reason analytically
- Demonstrate a working knowledge of microcomputers and generally utilized law office applications
- Demonstrate good organizational and time management skills

To achieve these goals, students complete courses such as Introduction to Legal Assisting, Techniques of Interview and Investigation, Legal Research and Writing, Advanced Legal Research and Writing, Business Law, and Computerized Legal Research. They also choose three specialty areas such as probate and estate planning, corporations, real estate, civil litigation, criminal litigation, and family law. General education classes in English composition, math, and other subjects are also required, along with support courses in business law and financial accounting.

For more details, contact:

St. Petersburg Junior College
P.O. Box 13489
St. Petersburg, Florida 33733
spcollege.edu

Eastern Kentucky University

Eastern Kentucky University boasts both a four-year bachelor's degree and a two-year associate degree program in the field. EKU graduates have landed jobs with employers including large and small law firms, government agencies, large corporations, banks, and insurance companies. Some operate their own paralegal offices on a freelance basis.

In the bachelor's program, students must complete forty credit hours in the major, twelve credits in subjects that are designated as supporting requirements, and fifty-one credits of general education requirements. The general education requirements may include courses in areas such as English, history, math and science, social science, or other areas. Requirements also include twenty-one credits of elective courses and four credits in specified areas, for a total of 128 credit hours.

Since it is designed to be completed in about half the time, the associate degree program has fewer requirements, especially in general studies and electives. To earn a degree, students must complete thirty-seven credit hours in the major and twenty-eight hours of supporting requirements (including general education courses), for a total of sixty-five credit hours.

For more information, contact:

Department of Government
Eastern Kentucky University
Richmond, Kentucky 40475
eku.edu

University of California, San Diego

Featuring a combination of practical skills and legal theory and analysis, this extension program emphasizes the working relationship between paralegals and attorneys. Courses cover areas such as legal research, writing, interviewing, and substantive and procedural law.

Students enrolling in this program must have either a bachelor's degree or an associate degree, complete an interview that measures oral skills, and complete a paralegal aptitude test that measures verbal, reading, and analytical skills.

Students may choose from a part-time or full-time study program. The full-time program takes about twelve weeks to complete and is offered three times a year in the fall, spring, and summer. The part-time program allows students to begin in September, January, March, or June.

For more information, contact:

University of California
Paralegal Program/UCSD Extension
La Jolla, California 92093
paralegal.ucsd.edu

Loyola University Chicago

Loyola University offers a postbaccalaureate certificate in paralegal studies as well as an undergraduate option. To earn the certificate, students complete twelve two-credit courses for a total of twenty-four credit hours. The minimum completion time is eight months (normally over a period of four eight-week terms); however, students may take longer to complete the program. The undergraduate option is available to advanced students enrolled in Loyola's bachelor's degree program in Organizational Development and Leadership.

Course Descriptions

While the two-credit per course format is a bit unusual, a look at Loyola's course descriptions can provide insights into the types of topics studied by paralegal students.

- **Introduction to Paralegal Studies.** This course provides an introduction to the function and sources of American law (including the U.S. Constitution), the American legal system, and legal practice, focusing on the role of the paralegal. Recent developments, especially with regard to regulatory proposals affecting paralegals, are emphasized.

The course also examines paralegal career issues. It is required of all students in their first semester of study.

- **Legal Research and Writing I.** Here students are introduced to the fundamentals of legal research and methods for locating, analyzing, and updating case law. Students learn how to use various reference books in the law library as well as the online services (LEXIS and WESTLAW).
- **Legal Research and Writing II.** This course, which is required, continues to explore the variety of legal reference sources. It focuses on locating, analyzing, and updating statutory and administrative law. The course also covers basic practices in legal correspondence.
- **Legal Research and Writing III.** The third required course in this sequence reviews legal research techniques and focuses on the development of basic research strategy. Students practice analyzing legal authority in case law and statutes and learn how to develop a legal argument. One or more research memoranda are assigned, and outlines and rewrites are required.
- **Legal Ethics.** This course focuses on the ethical considerations in the practice of law that paralegals are likely to encounter, especially the unauthorized practice of law, client confidentiality, and conflicts of interest. Attorney and paralegal ethical codes are examined. The ethics course is required of all students.
- **Basic Business Organizations and Contracts.** This required course introduces the principles of agency law and the six basic forms of business organizations: sole proprietorships, partnerships (general, registered limited liability, and limited), limited liability companies, and corporations. This course also covers the funda-

mentals of contract law, specifically contractual elements (contractual capacity, offer and acceptance, and consideration and legality and contractual intent) and standard contractual provisions.

- **Advanced Business Organizations.** This course continues the study of business organizations, focusing on the preparation of government-required forms, operating agreements, articles of incorporation and bylaws, consent forms, corporate minutes, annual reports, and so forth. Standard due diligence procedures for corporate transactions, including mergers and consolidations, are also covered.

- **Commercial Transactions I.** The major focus of this course is on typical commercial transactions, specifically those covered by Uniform Commercial Code Article 2 (Sales) and 2A (Leases). The Basic Business Organizations and Contracts course is a prerequisite.

- **Commercial Transactions II.** This course covers Uniform Commercial Code Article 9 (Secured Transactions) and federal bankruptcy law, including Chapter 7 liquidation proceedings and Chapters 11 and 13 reorganization plans.

- **Civil Litigation I.** This course introduces the civil litigation process in state (Illinois) and federal courts and proceedings in administrative agencies generally. Course content focuses on initial phases, including client interviews, prelitigation investigation, jurisdiction and venue considerations, filing a lawsuit, service of process, and the defendant's responsive pleadings.

- **Civil Litigation II.** The study of the litigation process is continued with the discovery, trial, and post-trial stages. Discovery topics include interrogatories, depositions, document production and inspection requests, physical and mental examinations, and requests for admission. Other topics include evidentiary issues, settlement negotiations, organization of case files, document control systems, trial preparation, trial procedure, and post-trial proceedings.

Overviews of administrative hearings and alternative dispute resolution are also presented.

- **Litigation III: Drafting of Pleadings.** This course focuses specifically on the preparation of pleadings for civil lawsuits. Material is covered from the initial complaint through post-trial motions and notices of appeal.
- **Real Estate Transactions I.** The content of this course proceeds from the concepts of real estate ownership to real estate sales transactions. Special emphasis is given to the preparation of documents required for residential real estate transactions: purchase and sale agreements, deeds and other closing documents, title insurance commitments, and policies and surveys.
- **Real Estate Transactions II.** Students who take this course continue the study of real estate transactions, examining issues that arise in commercial real estate transactions and especially the documentation of these transactions. Commercial real estate leasing is also covered.
- **Law Office Computer Applications.** This course develops practical skills through hands-on instruction in software programs commonly used in law offices: word processing (templates, redlining, and tables), spreadsheets (financial data, charts, and graphs), database management (organizing, sorting, and retrieving information), and presentation graphics.
- **Computer Applications for Litigation.** In completing this course, students develop practical skills through hands-on instruction in software programs commonly used for litigation support in law offices. Specific uses of word processing, spreadsheet, and database management software are practiced, followed by commercial litigation support programs such as Summation and Concordance. Online resources (court websites and docket searching programs, for example) are also examined.

- **Computer Applications for Legal Transactions.** This course develops practical skills through hands-on instruction in software programs commonly used in law offices to assist transactional work. Students practice specific uses of word processing, spreadsheet and database management software, as well as various commercial software programs. Online resources (public records and corporate information, for example) are also examined.
- **Advanced Legal Research and Writing.** This course provides additional experience in legal research and analysis, including both traditional and online resources. Students write memoranda in support of motions and study the mechanics of appellate briefs.
- **Torts.** The torts course introduces the fundamentals of civil tort liability, including intentional and quasi-intentional torts, negligence, strict liability, and product liability. The course focuses on the role of the paralegal in personal injury litigation from both the plaintiff's and defendant's viewpoints. The impact of insurance on tort litigation is also considered.
- **Medical Malpractice.** The focus of this course is on negligence lawsuits brought against health care organizations and health care professionals, from both the plaintiff's and defendant's viewpoints. The emphasis is on Illinois law and rules of procedure and on practical skills for locating and organizing medical information.
- **Intellectual Property: Patents and Trade Secrets.** This course introduces the terminology, basic principles, and documentation requirements of patent protection. Students examine the subject matter of patents, the concept of patentability, the patent application process, and patent infringement litigation. Trade secret misappropriation is also considered.
- **Intellectual Property: Trademarks and Copyrights.** This course introduces the terminology, basic principles, and documen-

tation requirements of trademark and copyright protection. Registration procedures and infringement disputes also are covered.

- **Securities Regulation I.** This course deals with the federal and state regulation of securities transactions. Students learn how the stock market works and the roles of brokers, specialists, and underwriters. The course focuses on the requirements for public offerings of stock, notably the registration statement and prospectus, as well as the antifraud provisions.
- **Securities Regulation II.** As a follow-up to the introductory course, this course deals with public trading registration, including reporting and disclosure requirements and Rule 10b-5. The course also examines state "blue sky" laws and registration procedures, emphasizing the Illinois Securities Act.
- **Estates, Trusts, and Wills I.** The basic principles of estate planning and estate and trust administration are covered in this course. It emphasizes the drafting of estate planning documents such as wills and trusts. Probate proceedings also are covered, including the preparation of probate court pleadings, collection and valuation of assets, review of claims, distribution of assets among beneficiaries, and accountings. An overview of tax considerations is also provided.
- **Estates, Trusts, and Wills II: Elder Law.** This course introduces a selection of legal topics that affect the elderly. These include long-term health care issues, Medicare and Medicaid planning, guardianships, health care proxies, advance directives, and ethical concerns.
- **Family Law.** The major topics covered in this course are the laws governing family relationships, specifically the Illinois Marriage and Dissolution of Marriage Act and related statutes. The course focuses on such practical aspects as investigation, prepara-

tion of pleadings and other documents, court procedures, settlement agreements, and postdecree modifications. A brief overview of adoption and paternity proceedings is also presented.

- **Criminal Law and Litigation.** This course examines the purpose and scope of substantive criminal law, considering topics such as the elements of various crimes against persons and property, criminal liability and punishment, and defenses to crimes. Procedural topics are also emphasized, including the preparation of court forms and pleadings commonly used in the criminal trial process. Illinois law is used to illustrate these topics.

- **Environmental Law.** Students learn about several major federal environmental statutes regulating air and water quality, waste management, and remediation of hazardous substances in this course. The focus is on issues leading to enforcement proceedings. Research strategies for this technical area are addressed.

- **Employment Law.** This course provides an overview of the legal relationship between employers and employees, including the employment-at-will doctrine, employment contracts, federal and state antidiscrimination laws, and worker's compensation proceedings. Administrative procedures as well as court actions are studied.

- **Immigration Law.** Here students learn about the federal immigration system, including the naturalization process and the rights and obligations of aliens in the United States. The preparation of visa applications is a major focus.

- **Internship.** In completing an internship, students gain practical experience (120 hours on-site) in applying paralegal skills within selected law firms, corporate law departments, and governmental agencies. Students keep a journal, participate in online discussions with other student interns, and write a report evaluating their experiences.

For more information about any of these courses or the overall program, contact:

Loyola University, Chicago
820 North Michigan Avenue
Lewis Towers 610
Chicago, Illinois 60611
paralegal.edu

Humber College

Canada's Humber College offers a bachelor of applied arts degree with a specialization in paralegal studies. Graduates develop skills in legal research, legal writing, evidence and advocacy, interviewing and investigation, negotiations, mediation and arbitration, professional ethics, and business entrepreneurship. Most students take eight semesters and one paid work term to complete the program.

The program includes courses in tort and contract law, landlord and tenant law, immigration and refugee law, debtor and creditor rights, and employment and labor law. Students develop a solid understanding of legal concepts, values, and principles integral to the Canadian legal system, along with analytical, research, problem solving, and communication skills.

Generally, the course of study is as follows:

Year One
Philosophy of Law
Introduction to Canada's Legal System
Small Claims Court 1
Small Claims Court 2
Tort and Contract Law

Psychology
Charter of Rights and Freedoms
Evidence
Introduction to Legal Writing
Political Science

Year Two
Law, Social Justice, and Human Rights
Administrative Tribunals
Legal History
Statistics
Sociology
Law, Family, and Gender
Legal Research
Landlord and Tenant
Provincial Offences
Microeconomics

Year Three
Immigration and Refugee Law
Advocacy
Negotiations and Mediation
Court and Government Office Administration
Career Development
Alternative Dispute Resolution
Debtor/Creditor Rights
Elder Law
Advanced Legal Writing
Electives
Paid Work Term

Year Four
Advanced Legal Issues
Tax and Accounting for Paralegals
Legal Framework of Business Enterprises
Professional Ethics
Access to Justice
Small Business Entrepreneurship
Insurance Law
Employment and Labor Law
Electives

For admission requirements, costs, and other information, contact:

Humber College, North Campus
205 Humber College Boulevard
Toronto, Ontario
 Canada M9W 5L7
humber.ca

Certification

Most employers of paralegals do not require special certification. Nevertheless, earning a voluntary certificate from a professional society may provide a boost in seeking employment or advancing on the job.

One source of certification is the National Association of Legal Assistants, which has developed standards for certification requiring specified combinations of education and experience. Paralegals who meet these standards may take a two-day examination, given three times each year at several regional testing centers. Paralegals who successfully complete this examination may use the designation Certified Legal Assistant (CLA).

For more information, contact:

National Association of Legal Assistants, Inc.
1516 South Boston Street, Suite 200
Tulsa, Oklahoma 74119
nala.org

Another provider of certification is the National Federation of Paralegal Associations, which has been offering the Paralegal Advanced Competency Exam since 1996. It offers professional recognition to paralegals who hold a bachelor's degree and have had at least two years of experience in the field. Once they successfully complete this examination, paralegals may use the designation of Registered Paralegal (RP).

More details are available from:

National Federation of Paralegal Associations
P.O. Box 33108
Kansas City, Missouri 64114
paralegals.org

There is some disagreement about the necessity of certification (see discussion in Chapter 8). Whether you will be interested is a matter that can be determined after you have gained some experience in the field.

Internships

Many legal-assistant education programs include an internship as a part of the curriculum. The internship enables a student to combine skills acquired in the program with practical on-the-job experience. Internships may take place in a variety of settings, including private law firms; offices of public defenders, public prosecutors, or attorneys general; banks; corporate legal departments; legal aid programs; government agencies; and other areas.

An example of an internship program is the program for summer interns sponsored by the Legal Services Corporation. Students earn $9 to $14 per hour while performing tasks needed by staff in this government-funded organization, which distributes federal funds to private legal aid programs across the country.

Candidates for internships are expected to have excellent editing and writing skills. They perform duties such as the following:

- Proofing and editing brief narratives prepared by staff
- Proofing and editing training guides, manuals, and instructions
- Writing and editing memos and reports
- Copying statistical data and text between automated applications
- Conducting Internet research
- Printing automated files
- Organizing files
- Mailing documents

For more information, contact:

Legal Services Corporation
3333 K Street NW, 3rd Floor
Washington, D.C. 20007
lsc.gov

Assessing a Paralegal Program

If you decide on a formal training program, what standards can you use to assess it? The American Bar Association (ABA) Committee on Legal Assistants has established some criteria for paralegal training programs. Based on meeting these criteria, schools are given ABA approval.

However, some authorities contend that the criteria for approval of schools is irrelevant to the work many paralegals—especially public service paralegals—perform. Even the ABA has noted: "The American Bar Association believes that there should be a number of ways in which a person can demonstrate competence as a legal assistant, one of which is the completion of an approved program. . . . It is not intended to limit entry into this career field by other means."

Seeking approval from the American Bar Association is a voluntary effort initiated by the institution offering the program. Therefore, a lack of ABA approval does not necessarily mean that the program being offered is not reputable. In addition, to be eligible for provisional approval, a program must be operational for at least one academic year. To be eligible for final approval, a program must be operational for at least two academic years and have graduated students.

Consider your needs. Remember why you plan to attend a paralegal training program. Certain schools or training programs that do not meet the American Bar Association's criteria may still be suitable for your needs.

The ABA has said that explicit objectives should be stated for specific programs. For example, a program should specify that when you are done, you will be qualified to get a position as a clerk of court or to handle real estate transactions under the supervision of a lawyer.

The program should have an advisory committee, including practicing lawyers, legal assistants from the public and private sectors, faculty and school administrators, and one or more members of the general public. A spokesperson for the National Paralegal Federation, a voluntary association of paralegals, has pointed out that the inclusion of practicing paralegals on the advisory committee and on the staff of the school may be especially important.

In the last decade, many new programs and schools have opened in the paralegal area. Some of them may not be financially sound, so prospective students could find themselves having paid their tuition but not having received adequate training. Check how long the school has been in operation and the reputation of its owners.

Be sure the school is accredited by the state in which it is operating. Does the local Better Business Bureau or chamber of commerce have any information on the school, including complaints filed against it?

Are you planning to work while you attend classes? If so, are classes offered at times that will allow you to work? This is an important factor to consider when selecting a program.

The Federal Trade Commission has issued regulations that require proprietary (private, for-profit) schools to disclose the placement rate for their graduates and their starting salaries. The FTC regulations do not apply to public schools, so students planning to attend public schools should try to get this information from the schools' placement offices. In some cases, proprietary schools may have a better placement record than public schools.

Also find out in advance what the program will cost. Be sure to ask specific questions. Does the amount published include all the costs for items such as tuition, books, laboratory fees, computer rentals, and other expenses? Does the program have to be paid for all at once, or is there a time-payment plan? Are student loans or other financial aid available? What steps must you take to apply for financial assistance? Be sure to ask questions well in advance of enrolling at any school. Not only should such factors be a major consideration in your choice, but advance deadlines may apply.

Computer Training

Modern paralegals use computers extensively in their work. Computer software packages and online research techniques are frequently used to search legal literature stored in computer databases and on CD-ROMs or other electronic storage media. In litigation that involves many supporting documents, paralegals use computers to organize and index the material. They also may use computer software packages to perform tax computations and explore the consequences of possible tax strategies for clients.

Paralegals using general business systems, such as spreadsheets and database management programs, are able to perform complex analyses to support litigation work in tax, corporate law, estate, real estate, as well as in many other areas.

Paralegals with computer training can search electronic databases, manage electronic mail systems, and perform other research. Some paralegals act as in-house consultants, helping to develop new applications and training professional and support staff in routine uses of the computer.

Because of the time saving and efficiency of computers, paralegals need to have a strong foundation in computer literacy and usage. The more you know and can do, the more valuable you can become.

In general, it is wise from a career viewpoint to develop as much knowledge as possible about computer applications in the legal office or other settings where paralegals operate. The ability to keep up with changing office technologies and assist attorneys or other supervisors in selecting, operating, or updating computer equipment and software can enhance your job and career advancement prospects.

4

Private Versus Public Sector Employment

Paralegals work for a variety of employers. Some employers operate as private businesses. Others function on a nonprofit basis. Although similar job skills are involved, there may be some important differences for paralegals working in the two sectors.

The Private Sector

Private law firms employ more paralegals than any other type of organization. Since they depend on the funds paid by clients to stay in operation, they fit squarely within what is known as the private sector, or the part of the economy that operates on a profit-making basis. By their very nature, a primary purpose of private law firms is to generate income. But at the same time, they provide important services for the individuals and organizations they serve. They also provide some free or "pro bono" services to needy clients.

Despite their importance, law firms are not the only private sector organizations that employ paralegals. A variety of firms ranging from banks and insurance companies to large manufacturing or retail corporations also depend on the work of paralegals. These employees may be called insurance adjusters, life insurance underwriters, or booking and contract agents for athletes, entertainers, and writers. Or they may be classified by various titles as employees of escrow and title companies or as employees in many banks and savings and loan institutions. An illustration of this type of employer is a California bank that hired eighty new paralegals in one year.

In large urban areas, paralegal jobs in the private sector tend to cluster around litigation, corporate work, estate planning, and probate. Paralegals also are employed in contract work, employee benefits, criminal law, real estate, worker's compensation, bankruptcy, labor law, domestic relations (family law), appellate work, and in general-practice firms.

In both corporations and private firms, most paralegals tend to specialize. However, some firms employ paralegal generalists who understand and can work in two or three of the firm's specialties. The paralegal generalist most often is employed in a small firm.

Another trend is for freelance paralegals to establish their own firms.

Corporate Law

One opportune area for the paralegal in the private sector is corporate law. The corporate field generally includes all legal problems of businesses other than lawsuits. A paralegal in this practice area may be responsible for preparing articles of incorporation, maintaining corporate minutes, developing information for the establishment of pension and profit-sharing plans, and other administrative problems.

Individuals with a background in this area may be able to find employment in the legal departments of corporations as well as in private law firms.

Those best equipped for success in this area should have good academic records and excellent writing skills. Solid organizational skills are also a must. Many lawyers have found that paralegals who possess these skills and the necessary training can deal as effectively as attorneys in carrying out some tasks.

A newly hired paralegal may be used to maintain a corporate tickler or docket so that a lawyer stays on top of corporate timetables or filing requirements. Other work might include arranging meetings, filling out forms and reports, and writing minutes of meetings. The paralegal might be assigned to complete a variety of tasks such as preparing preliminary drafts of notices, taking corporate minutes, drafting agreements or portions of agreements, and developing initial drafts of applications and reports to regulatory authorities.

After gaining more experience, the paralegal may work with less direct supervision and function as an integral member of the legal team. This may include increased levels of contact with both lawyers and clients.

Litigation

Litigation involves civil disputes resolved through the courts in lawsuits. Paralegals involved in litigation, most of whom are employed by private law firms, conduct legal research. This work may include shepherding cases, writing briefs, or performing background research.

Some paralegals do legislative history to check on the background of specific legislation dealing with real estate law. Other paralegals draft preliminary answers to written interrogatories or draft preliminary interrogatories for the opposing attorney.

Other general duties include maintaining an office "tickler" system and an individual attorney's calendar. Frequently, the paralegal is in charge of the client's complete file—opening it, keeping it up to date, and knowing where different parts of it are at all times. Experienced paralegals may train other staff members in the office procedures involved in handling cases.

Estate Planning and Probate

Many paralegals handle estate planning and probate. This field involves the planning and administration of estates and trusts. A paralegal in this area of practice may be responsible for interviewing clients, drafting wills, preparing inventories of estates, preparing documents to be filed in probate court, and doing tax work. A background in tax and accounting is helpful.

Real Estate

Firms specializing in real estate often employ paralegals. In this work, paralegal staff may follow a form manual. This manual, like a cookbook, spells out the steps to follow in handling cases. Paralegals may be hired by a firm to produce such a manual. Often specific forms must be filled out. In some ways, this is more repetitious work than in most other types of law practice.

Typically, the paralegal interviews clients and obtains and records basic information on the real estate transaction. This work usually occurs after the lawyer speaks to the client. For a real estate sale, the paralegal, using a checklist, asks the client the names and addresses of present mortgage holders, the date of original purchase, capital improvements made on the structure, and similar questions.

Some paralegals help attorneys with title work. This may involve conducting a title search in the records office or preparing a preliminary abstract of title for the attorney. More commonly, the paralegal will arrange for the purchase of title insurance. In mortgage work, the paralegal may assist a client in obtaining mortgage financing, review a client's mortgage applications, or assist in the recording of mortgages.

Most paralegals in the real estate area assist with closings. They may arrange for the closing date, notify all parties involved, record minutes of the closing, be a general aide to the attorney, and notarize documents. Paralegals may assist the client in obtaining a mortgage and homeowner's policy or coordinate the office's handling of insurance claims of the client.

Career Advancement

A firm's philosophy regarding paralegals will affect its use of paralegals. If the paralegal is thought to be capable and intelligent, secretarial and clerical help will be advanced to this individual. A firm that simply wants to spare its attorneys repetitious or time-consuming tasks probably does not understand how valuable a paralegal can be and may burden the paralegal with secretarial or bookkeeping duties.

Understand what a firm expects of you before you begin. Paralegals starting out may have to accept less-than-perfect conditions just to gain experience. They should then be alert to the possibility of educating their employer as to their potential; if this is not feasible, they should seek a better position in another place.

Freelance Paralegals

Some brave individuals have opened up their own paralegal practices. They have become entrepreneurs. Many of their clients are attorneys, although they may also work for nonlawyers in corporations or banks handling probate, pensions and benefits, or real estate titles.

The successful freelance paralegals suggest that before choosing this career path, an individual should get experience for at least three to five years and build up a reputation for solid work consistently performed. "It is vital to build up a network of prior employers who respect your skills a lot and will use you when you go freelance," says one such professional.

As with any business, there are risks involved in setting up an office and seeking clients. Consequently, some paralegals freelance on a limited basis while retaining their regular position. Then, as their business grows, they can quit their job and expect to be reasonably solvent.

Some paralegals get their business established and only then invest heavily in word processing and computer equipment. Many freelance paralegals begin working out of their homes and gradually move out of their houses as their businesses become successful.

Being in any business often demands hard work and long hours. A paralegal business is no exception. It also requires good time management skills, a high level of motivation, and patience in developing business leads and attracting clients.

The Public Sector

Legal services can be very expensive. While the rich and well connected can easily afford to hire attorneys, the same is not true for the poor. Even for many in the middle class, the costs of legal representation can be out of reach. Children, immigrants, those with mental disabilities, and the elderly often face challenges in obtaining legal services. Other groups, such as citizens concerned with problems such as environmental pollution and/or the rights of prisoners, may lack access to legal services.

To combat this problem, several remedies have been developed. Many of the solutions rely heavily on the use of paralegals. The employment of paralegals helps keep costs down. Paralegals (whether or not they are members of the groups being served) provide an effective link with individuals or groups seeking help.

The Scope of Public Sector Law

As previously noted, private sector law includes those services selected and fully paid for by individuals or corporate clients. This is the traditional scope of law practice. By contrast, public sector law includes legal problems generally not handled by private attorneys or government agencies. It also includes poverty law and other consumer advocacy services in which the clients do not expect to pay the full cost of their representation.

Although circumstances vary, public sector employers often have more limited resources than those in the private sector. As a result, they may pay lower salaries or offer more spartan working conditions than many private employers. Benefits such as profit sharing are not part of the employment package. For those who work in the public sector, the satisfaction of helping those in need is often seen as a compensating factor.

Group Legal Services

In recent years, with prepaid legal services plans or group legal services, the distinction between public sector and private sector law has become less clear than it once was.

With prepaid legal services plans, an individual usually pays a monthly set fee similar to a health insurance premium. The services one can expect to receive free or at a special group rate may include initial consultation, wills, consumer problems, family and real estate matters, bankruptcies, and tax representation. Paralegals often improve the assistance received by those unfamiliar with the legal process by directing them to the appropriate services available to handle their problems.

The paralegal interviews the client and discovers the nature of the problem to be addressed. Quite often, the paralegal can handle the problem. If it is a complex legal issue, however, the paralegal may draft a memorandum to the lawyer describing the case and outlining the options.

If the case involves an administrative hearing, the paralegal asks the clients for details and supporting evidence. Then the paralegal might accompany and represent the client before the administrative hearing. The paralegal may turn the client over to another paralegal who is a specialist or who practices before a particular administrative agency.

Public Sector Employers

A typical public sector employer that utilizes paralegals in a number of roles is the Legal Services Corporation, a nonprofit corporation established by Congress to provide low-cost legal help to poor people. In addition, state and local organizations also employ paralegals to serve their constituencies.

Public sector nonprofit agencies sometimes hire by word of mouth. To get a job in a public sector agency, one may not go through a school or a placement agency. Some jobs in a public sector agency are obtained by knowing someone in the agency or by seeking out the director of the agency and convincing that person that you have the skills and background needed to serve the type of client coming for help.

Quite often, public sector paralegals have greater opportunity to do a wider variety of tasks than paralegals in the private sector. They may also work more closely with clients.

Many public sector paralegals do not work directly under the supervision of a lawyer. Sometimes this has led to conflict with the state laws about unauthorized legal practice. Public sector paralegals activities include outreach work, advocacy, and representation of clients before administrative agencies.

Public sector paralegals may be unaffiliated with attorney-controlled organizations. They may work instead for groups of senior citizens, tenants, welfare recipients, or others. A challenging area of law is public interest advocacy—helping people gain the rights promised them as part of a democratic government.

Types of Positions

Public sector paralegals function in a number of ways. They may do outreach work to let people know about organizations that represent them and their interests. Some paralegals raise funds to sustain their organizations. Most paralegals interview clients and make referrals to other agencies where clients can get more suitable or additional help. They often write up their introductory interview with the prospective client and present it to the supervising attorney. Some paralegals may brief their attorneys orally and introduce the client to them.

Later, paralegals may research the issues involved and write up this research for the attorney's use in drafting pleadings. Paralegals might draft the pleadings themselves. Other paralegals are in charge of public relations and write drafts about issues involved for relevant newsletters or mass media exposure. A few paralegals serve as contact persons for the print or broadcast media.

If a settlement is possible, paralegals might serve as arbitrators. Paralegals also can serve in other functions, such as arranging for expert or character witnesses and helping prepare witnesses for their testimony if a case goes to trial. They also can ensure that there is no conflict in the scheduled court date for client, attorney, or witnesses. Although paralegals cannot represent clients in trials, they may represent them at administrative hearings.

Job Titles and Responsibilities

Paralegals in the public sector have a variety of job titles. They may perform a wide range of duties.

Most paralegals employed in programs funded by the Legal Services Corporation interview clients. Many also do legal research and draft legal documents. Some do investigative work. They may also negotiate with government agencies on behalf of clients in public entitlement cases or represent clients at administrative hearings.

Public sector paralegals have reported the following job titles: administrator, community worker, counselor, debt counselor, Indian/tribal advocate, intake interviewer/clerk, interviewer, investigator, legal intern/law student, paralegal, secretary/clerk/office manager, and others.

Legal Clinics

One program funded by the Legal Services Corporation is the staff legal clinic. This approach involves a core of attorneys supplemented by paralegals, law students, lay workers, and others. The staff uses such techniques as standardized forms, machine processing, computerized support systems, and self-help education. The legal clinic approach appeals to both poor and middle-class people.

Paralegals determine initial eligibility and then schedule an appointment for an intake interview. During this interview, final eligibility is determined, and the nature of the legal problem is recorded on the intake form.

Paralegals typically spend thirty to forty minutes on each intake interview. This time is necessary because clients very often have nonlegal problems for which they need counseling or referral to other social service agencies. For example, paralegals may provide instruction in such matters as government-assistance regulations.

Administrative Hearings

Within the Legal Services Corporation, some paralegals work with relative independence on administrative hearings, as permitted by law. For example, Legal Services projects may establish a welfare hearing division staffed primarily by paralegals who are authorized under the federal regulations to represent clients at hearings. The paralegals who perform in this way may be called advocacy paralegals. The majority of Legal Services paralegals perform client representation at administrative hearings as part of their work.

For more information, contact:

Legal Services Corporation
3333 K Street NW, 3rd Floor
Washington, D.C. 20007-3522
lsc.gov

Outreach Work

Public sector paralegals may solicit clients to inform them of any
legal help that they may need or to which they are entitled. This
outreach work is often necessary in the public sector since many
people living in poverty areas are poorly informed about their rights
and about available legal help. Unless outreach work is done, these
people may not be served.

Community service advisors and paralegals are especially important to the elderly. A great number of elderly people live in poverty
because they are unaware of public benefits programs to which they
are entitled. Outreach is critical to them.

Some paralegals are also members of the advocacy groups they
represent. In these dual roles, they can make sure the groups receive
the legal services they need. At the same time, they can help reduce
the costs that must be incurred by the organizations.

Opportunities for All

In many cases, public sector organizations place a great deal of
emphasis on being equal opportunity employers. They employ large
numbers of women as well as men. In addition, public sector paralegals come from a wide range of educational, cultural, and racial
backgrounds.

To obtain employment, job applicants must demonstrate intelligence and the capacity to do the work. They tend to have good

verbal ability and extensive experience in the life problems they service. Many public sector paralegals are from racial minorities. Increasing attention has recently been paid to the use of senior citizens as paralegals. Senior citizens often make very effective paralegals for serving the needs of the elderly poor.

Once employed, paralegals who work in the public sector may gain valuable experience. Public sector work offers direct client contact and responsibility for the work product. That kind of contact and responsibility is rare in private law firms.

Volunteer Opportunities

Some paralegals have gotten valuable experience serving as volunteers to public interest groups. This work enabled them to see the operation of offices firsthand and decide if the work was interesting enough to pursue as a career. In a few cases, the volunteer paralegals could not be hired as paid employees because the organization did not have enough money to pay for their services.

Sample Volunteer Program

Probono.net/dc is a joint project of the Washington, D.C., Consortium of Legal Service Providers and the D.C. Bar Pro Bono Program. This virtual public interest law community uses the Internet, e-mail, and other technology resources to increase the amount and quality of legal services provided to low-income citizens, nonprofit organizations, and small, disadvantaged businesses. Along with lawyers and law students, the group provides opportunities for paralegals to offer volunteer services ranging from telephone intake to case development in landlord-tenant and family law cases. Organizations that have requested volunteers for such services have included the following:

- Archdiocesan Legal Network for Catholic Charities
- Bread for the City
- Covenant House Washington, Division of Legal Services
- D.C. Association for Retarded Citizens
- D.C. Bar Pro Bono Program
- Lawyers for Children America
- Legal Aid Society of the District of Columbia
- Legal Counsel for the Elderly
- Legal Services of Northern Virginia
- Multi-Door Dispute Resolution Division (alternative dispute resolution)
- Washington Legal Clinic for the Homeless
- Whitman-Walker Clinic
- Women Empowered Against Violence, Inc.

For more information, check the organization's website at probono .net/dc.

Helping Low-Income Families

An example of a local group concerned with the legal rights of those with limited resources is the Economic Justice Institute of Madison, Wisconsin. Formerly known as the Center for Public Representation, the institute assists consumers and low-income families through education, research, training, and representation. EJI operates a Neighborhood Law Project, a Consumer Law Litigation Clinic, and an Elder Law Clinic.

For more information, contact:

Economic Justice Institute, Inc.
975 Bascom Mall
Madison, Wisconsin 53706
law.wisc.edu

5

Government Employment

A VARIETY OF government agencies employ paralegals who perform work not greatly unlike that in the private sector. Other paralegal-type governmental jobs include affirmative action officers, claims workers, many types of investigators and referees, hearing officers, mediators and conciliators, and contract officers and procurement specialists.

Federal Government Jobs

The federal government is the largest single employer in the United States. As such, it offers an attractive range of positions to those who seek employment as paralegals. Federal government jobs offer well-defined paths of career advancement, exceptional job security, and, in many cases, generous pension plans and retirement benefits.

Applying for a Position

The federal government employs paralegals at several levels of responsibility and salary. Positions may be available in a variety of agencies.

Applicants for federal government jobs now apply by submitting an ordinary résumé, the Optional Application for Federal Employment (form OF-612), or any other written format of choice. In some cases (such as when electronic application processing systems are used or when jobs require special skills), other specialized application forms may be required.

Federal Jobs Site

To learn more about government jobs, check out the website maintained by the United States Office of Personnel Management, usajobs.com. The Feds tout this as "the Federal Government's official one-stop source for federal jobs and employment information."

At this site you can search a database of more than eighteen thousand federal jobs, create and store an electronic copy of a résumé for applying to government jobs, and set up your own free online account to post résumés, attract employers, and have job information e-mailed to you. You can also review a selection of frequently asked questions and review information and advice about obtaining a government job.

For more information, check out this site at usajobs.opm.gov.

Canadian Government Jobs Site

A comprehensive jobs site is also operated by the Canadian government. It includes links to listings of jobs with the federal government, provincial and territorial governments and municipal governments, as well as to local offices of interest to jobseekers. The site also includes information for aboriginal persons, newcomers to Canada, non-Canadians, persons with disabilities, and youth.

You can explore this site at jobsetc.ca.

Private Sources of Job Information

In addition to government-sponsored job sites, private companies may also be useful in the job search process.

For example, Federal Research Service has been a leading source of federal job information since 1974. It offers a free monthly electronic newsletter, "FedJobs Career Chat," a publication called *Federal Career Opportunities*, and a variety of services, some of which are fee-based. Attractive features include targeted job searches, automatic e-mail alerts of job opportunities, application forms, how-to booklets, and a comprehensive library of articles and resources on finding and landing federal government jobs.

Users can search the job database by occupational groups or series, state or region, federal agency, GS grade level, salary range, or time frame of listing.

For more information, contact:

Federal Research Service
P.O. Box 1708
Annandale, Virginia 22003
fedjobs.com

Factors Influencing Hiring Decisions

Most U.S. government jobs are ranked according to levels, called "GS" (for government service). Paralegal positions generally range from GS-5 to GS-9 and occasionally to GS-12.

The federal government uses a number of factors in judging a potential paralegal's competence and grade-level status. Knowing what these standards encompass should enable you to develop an effective application. These factors are arranged to provide for low to advanced levels of paraprofessional skills and illustrate the hierarchy of positions paralegals may hold. Additionally, descriptions may be instructive for those not contemplating federal government careers but who are interested in learning what paralegals do.

When filling out your federal government application, be sure to address each of the factors. If there is insufficient room on your application, use extra sheets.

Knowledge Required

At the most basic level, typical work involves dealing with agency regulations, laws, and court opinions. Necessary skills include the ability to be analytical, to interview, to give a clear presentation of the facts, to perform developmental assignments, and to rapidly learn the technical work.

At the next higher level, candidates will be able to apply basic legal principles, concepts, and practices and independently perform data analysis. At this stage, an applicant should know how to do legal research and how to use references such as agency manuals, electronic databases, directives, court reports, and appellate records in commercial-legal publications. Using these references, a paralegal should be able to locate needed information such as applicable precedents, legislative history, and commentaries that are pertinent to the legal issue.

At the next level, paralegals should know and be able to use legal techniques and skills to analyze both issues of facts and law, to digest decisions, to evaluate applicability of precedents, and to draft briefs and other litigation papers, including advisory opinions and findings. Paralegals also should know formal and informal rules of evidence and have the skills necessary to evaluate the adequacy and/or admissibility of evidence, to request additional data or further investigation, to develop narrative or graphic exhibits, and to support specified legal arguments.

Then, continuing up the grade level, paralegals should have additional knowledge and skills. This includes application of various laws, court and administrative decisions, interpretations of rules and regulations, policies, and procedures that pertain to the administration of particular legal programs (for example, communications or antitrust) to particular types of legal cases (such as civil or criminal cases investigated and prosecuted by a U.S. attorney's office). Other duties are analysis of the relevance of particular technical evidence on questions that arise in specialized legal programs. Paralegals should be able to perform extensive legal research into the legislative history, precedent, and other applicable decisions and opinions. They should be able to investigate and have familiarity with the subject-matter details of a case or the legal matters to determine the best approaches to obtain relevant data and have enough financial or statistical data.

Supervisory Control and Use of Guidelines

At each successively higher level, there is less direct supervision as the person is able to work more independently.

Complexity

Complications arise from program issues such as physical disability, industrial practices, labor market considerations, questions of ecology, and public communication needs. Again, as you might suspect, complexity increases as one progresses higher up the scale.

Scope and Effect

This area covers the relationship between the nature of the work (the purpose, breadth, and depth of the assignments) and the effect (the work products or services). Here, paralegal work largely involves the performance of specific, routine, and repetitive operations with occasional demands to look for factual information in subpoenaed documents and to tabulate data or to review recent case decisions and summarize the factual legal issues and findings.

At a more advanced level, the duties are to carry out specific parts of a procedure such as initially reviewing formal complaints, identifying issues involved, and obtaining the information and documentation to prepare the case for analysis and development by other paralegal specialists or professional staff; or analyzing documents for supportive evidence, organizing findings, and writing synopses for use by an attorney.

The work in the step beyond this is to resolve problems or questions through application of established criteria and methods such as reviewing matters to determine agency position in similar cases, deciding on and carrying out the necessary procedural steps, and recommending and justifying the need to take action such as litigation.

Beyond the previous step, the work is to advise others on highly specialized problems of case development, interpret findings or documentation requirements, monitor the consistency of case decisions throughout the agency, recommend the reopening of cases, or research unsettled issues and develop proposed agency positions. The work provides the foundation for precedents that have a broad impact, including affecting agency-wide ideas, programs, or activities of a regulated industry.

Related Positions

In addition to paralegal specialist positions, there are other government positions for which you may be eligible. These include the legal and kindred group, copyright patent and trademark group, legal clerk and technical claims examining series, legal instruments examiner, investigation group, equal opportunity compliance, consumer safety commission, and legal specialization of the technical writer/editor.

In some cases, government agencies promote from a lower-level position into an entry-level paralegal position. Therefore, persons with little legal experience or without a college degree may want to enter government service at a lower-level position and work toward gradual promotions.

Requirements and Responsibilities

The majority of federal government paralegal positions are located in the Departments of Justice, Treasury, and Defense (all branches), as well as in the various regulatory agencies. Many of these positions involve application of substantial legal knowledge working in support of attorneys or administrative law judges. The extent of legal education is used as a factor in ranking candidates.

Experience and Training

The federal government requires both general and specialized experience. This may be confusing to new applicants.

General experience is "progressively responsible experience which demonstrates the ability to explain, apply, or interpret rules, regulations, procedures, policies, precedents, or other kinds of criteria. This experience may have been gained in administrative, professional, investigative, technical, high-level clerical, or responsible work."

Qualifying general experience may have been gained as a legal clerk, claims examiner, claims adjuster, voucher examiner, investigator, or contract representative.

Specialized experience is "legal, quasi-legal, paralegal, legal technician, or related work that demonstrates an ability to evaluate pertinent facts and evidence; an ability to interpret and apply laws, rules, regulations, and precedents; skill and judgment in the analysis of cases; an ability to communicate effectively orally and in writing; and, as required, an ability to deal effectively with individuals and groups and knowledge of the pertinent subject area."

Opportunities for Persons with Disabilities

Men and women with disabilities may be eligible for some paralegal positions. Generally, job candidates must be physically able to perform the duties of the position efficiently and without hazard to themselves or to others. Ability to read without strain printed materials the size of typewritten characters is required, corrective lenses permitted. Ability to speak without impediment may be required for some positions. Ability to hear the conversational voice, with or without a hearing aid, is required for most positions; however, some positions may be suitable for the deaf. Candidates must possess emotional and mental stability.

State, Provincial, and Local Government Positions

State, provincial, and local governments also employ paralegals. Some states and municipalities have civil service classifications based on merit. In other cases, recommendation by a local or state politician gives the job candidate a definite edge. Do not be afraid to inform your elected representatives of your job plans and ask if they will recommend you to the hiring agency. It may not land you the job, but it can't hurt.

State and Provincial Government Personnel Agencies

Use the following Internet resources to search for state and provincial government positions in your area.

United States

Alabama Personnel Department
personnel.state.al.us

Alaska Job Center Network
Alaska Department of Labor and Workforce Development
jobs.state.ak.us

Arizona Human Resources
hr.state.az.us

Arkansas Office of Personnel Management
arkansas.gov/dfa/opm

California Department of Personnel Administration
dpa.ca.gov

California State Personnel Board
spb.ca.gov

Colorado Department of Personnel
colorado.gov/dpa

Connecticut Department of Administrative Services
das.state.ct.us

Delaware State Personnel Office
http://delawarepersonnel.com

Florida Human Resource Management
http://dms.myflorida.com/workforce/human_resource_management

Georgia Merit System
gms.state.ga.us

Hawaii Department of Human Resources Development
state.hi.us/hrd

Idaho Division of Human Resources
dhr.idaho.gov

Illinois Central Management Services
state.il.us/cms/persnl

Indiana Department of Personnel
in.gov/jobs

Iowa Department of Personnel
state.ia.us/government/idop

Kansas Department of Personnel
http://da.state.ks.us/ps

Kentucky Personnel Cabinet
http://personnel.ky.gov

Louisiana Department of State Civil Service
dscs.state.la.us

Maine Bureau of Human Resources
state.me.us/bhr

Maryland Office of Personnel Services and Benefits
dbm.maryland.gov

Massachusetts Human Resources Division
mass.gov/hrd

Michigan Department of Civil Service
michigan.gov/mdcs

Minnesota Department of Employee Relations
doer.state.mn.us

Mississippi State Personnel Board
spb.state.ms.us

Missouri Division of Personnel
oa.state.mo.us/pers

Montana State Personnel Division
discoveringmontana.com/doa

Nebraska DAS State Personnel Division
das.state.ne.us/personnel

Nevada Department of Personnel
http://dop.nv.gov

New Hampshire Division of Personnel
http://admin.state.nh.us

New Jersey Department of Personnel
state.nj.us/personnel

New Mexico State Personnel Office
state.nm.us/spo

New York Department of Civil Service
cs.state.ny.us

North Carolina Office of State Personnel
osp.state.nc.us

North Dakota Central Personnel Division
state.nd.us/hrms

Ohio Department of Administrative Services
http://das.ohio.gov/hrd

Oklahoma Office of Personnel Management
opm.state.ok.us

Oregon Human Resource Services Division
oregon.gov/das/hr

Pennsylvania Governor's Office of Administration, Human
    Resources, and Management
hrm.state.pa.us/oahrm

Rhode Island Office of Personnel Administration
http://controller.doa.state.ri.us

South Carolina Office of Human Resources
state.sc.us/ohr

South Dakota Bureau of Personnel
state.sd.us/bop/bop

Tennessee Department of Personnel
state.tn.us/personnel

Texas Human Resources
hr.state.tx.us

Utah Department of Human Resource Management
dhrm.state.ut.us

Vermont Department of Personnel
vermontpersonnel.org

Virginia Department of Human Resource Management
dpt.state.va.us

Washington Department of Personnel
http://hr.dop.wa.gov

West Virginia Division of Personnel
state.wv.us/admin/personnel

Wisconsin Office of State Employment Relations
http://oser.state.wi.us

Wyoming Human Resources Division
http://personnel.state.wy.us

Canada

Government of Alberta
pao.gov.ab.ca

Province of British Columbia
gov.bc.ca/bvprd/bc/home.do

Province of Manitoba
gov.mb.ca/csc/employment/jobs

Government of New Brunswick
gnb.ca

Government of Newfoundland and Labrador
gov.nf.ca

Government of the Northwest Territories
gov.nt.ca

Government of Nova Scotia
gov.ns.ca

Government of Nunavut
gov.nu.ca/nunavut

Government of Ontario
gov.on.ca

Government of Prince Edward Island
gov.pe.ca

Government of Quebec
gov.qc.ca

Government of Saskatchewan
gov.sk.ca

Government of Yukon
gov.yk.ca

Working for the Attorney General

Paralegal positions are found in most offices of state attorneys general and district attorneys. Jobs in these offices are varied. Duties may include the following: intake of arrest cases, case review, police liaison, diversion, and intake and follow-up of citizen-initiated cases, including citizen complaints. Responsibilities often involve handling various aspects of cases involving consumer fraud, non-support, and bad checks. Other responsibilities include case processing, calendaring, witness liaison, and trial preparation. Paralegals also may prepare bail forfeiture petitions; discuss bail review, extradition, and detainers; and handle habitual traffic offenders or parole revocation appeals.

In addition to these paralegal duties, there are also administrative and planning duties in the prosecutor's office. These may include the job of the budget or fiscal officer, who keeps track of expenditures and plans future budgets, or the nonlawyer personnel director.

Often, the personnel or human resources director serves as a trainer to both the attorneys and paralegals, explaining how to use the paralegals most efficiently. The personnel director in this situation, just as in many private law firms, reviews the type and amount of work assigned to each unit's staff and recommends changes where necessary. The personnel director, who may be a paralegal, often has the authority to hire and fire nonlawyers on the staff to ensure that the office runs smoothly and efficiently. The personnel director is also in charge of fringe benefits and carrying out the equal employment opportunity/affirmative action laws and regulations. He or she also may be charged with the upkeep of an office procedures manual.

Some attorneys general employ organized crime analysts who study criminal intelligence, analyze statistics, and then draw conclusions about the patterns of organized criminal activity.

Almost all attorneys general employ investigators who are assigned to such areas as consumer protection and organized crime control.

Working for the District Attorney

Paralegals also are used in district attorneys' offices. In some offices, they focus on the postindictment preparation of felony cases. In others, they deal with nonsupport cases, intake of arrest cases (including helping prosecutors screen out inappropriate arrest cases), development of prosecution charges, or identification of cases warranting special attention. Paralegals can help prosecutors administer a screening unit. With experience, paralegals may themselves perform a limited amount of screening and complaint drafting, subject to the review of a senior prosecutor.

Following are representative duties involved in intake of arrest cases:

- Log all incoming cases, noting the officer(s), defendant(s), arrest charge(s), and charges filed, if any.
- Check police officer's forms and records to ensure that a rap sheet and all necessary papers are assembled.
- Make sure the officer fills out an internal office report.
- Fill out the form giving information on witnesses' availability and how to contact them.
- Ensure a background check is made for detainees and outstanding warrants against each arrestee.
- Check the dispositions of earlier cases indicated on the arrestee's rap sheet.
- Route the officer and witnesses, if any, to the next available and appropriate district attorney.
- Prepare monthly statistical reports on cases entering the office filed without charges reduced, the number filed with charges reduced, cases returned for further investigation, and those in which prosecution was declined.

Paralegals also are engaged in police liaison, where they work closely with law enforcement officers. A paralegal reviews cases submitted to the district attorney, suggests investigative leads and techniques, and performs troubleshooting between the two agencies. This position is usually held by experienced and respected police officers who have retired or by people with strong public relations skills. The main job qualification is to understand the district attorney's needs and have the skills to translate those needs to the working police officers. Knowledge and skill in investigating crimes also is necessary but not mandatory.

Another job of the paralegal is diversion. Here, the paralegal helps to identify arrestees eligible for informal or formal programs that divert their cases out of the criminal justice system. The paralegal monitors adherence to the conditions of the diversion. Diversion includes a variety of social services, including job training and rehabilitation. This paralegal position is especially suitable for rehabilitation counseling majors or social work majors because it requires extensive contacts with rehabilitation, social service, and criminal justice planning agencies.

Another typical paralegal job in the district attorney's office is the handling of citizen complaints. The paralegal interviews citizens seeking the prosecution of alleged wrongdoers. The paralegal then refers their cases to appropriate agencies or conducts a mediation hearing between the disputants.

Many requests for prosecution come from citizens complaining about misconduct of family members, neighbors, landlords, or merchants. The wrongdoing is usually minor, and there is little objective evidence. Many of these cases are diverted into family court, to a police detective bureau, to small claims court, to legal aid, or to other community services outside of the formal justice system.

In the cases that are not diverted, the paralegal helps the parties go through an informal hearing to work out a settlement of the problem underlying the dispute. The first step is interviewing the complainant. Then a case file must be established. Names of complainants and respondents must be checked to see if they have been involved in other cases. After this, the case must be referred to the proper authority unless the paralegal determines that it should be resolved through arbitration or mediation. If this route is chosen and the complainant agrees, the paralegal should schedule a hearing date and notify the respondent.

Handling of citizen complaints is a high-level, stress-filled position. The paralegal often deals with family and neighborhood conflicts. A person with a social work or professional education background might be well suited for this position.

Paralegals in the district attorney's office may work in trial preparation. A major duty of these paralegals is following a checklist to ensure that all necessary papers are in the case file, such as the preliminary hearing transcript and police and lab reports. The paralegal handles telephone calls from police officers and lay witnesses and relays the attorney's response. He or she also prepares a list of potential witnesses, how they may be contacted, and to what they can testify.

The paralegal may contact potential witnesses and report their statements to the prosecutor to determine if the prosecutor wants to interview them. The paralegal will assist the prosecutor in identifying and having on file defendant and witness statements, exculpatory evidence, or other items that may have to be shown to the defense counsel.

Advanced paralegals working in this area have been permitted to deal with police officers and investigators directly. These paralegals debrief them on what they have learned, on what they have written down, and to what they can testify. They also may deal with lay witnesses and join the prosecutor in conducting witness conferences and interviews.

The paralegal also may function as a sounding board for the attorney in working through the trial strategy and the theory of the case. Some paralegals perform legal research for the attorney.

6

EARNINGS AND BENEFITS

IN ADDITION TO the work itself, salary and benefits are important considerations in evaluating where you would like to work. These can vary widely among different employers.

Compensation

Many paralegals believe that they are underpaid. In regions where there are more paralegals than available jobs, the excess number of paralegals tends to inhibit growth in salaries, especially for entry-level positions. In addition, a lack of appropriate recognition causes many attorneys to undervalue the contributions of paralegals.

What kind of income can a paralegal expect to earn? More so than in many fields, earnings vary greatly. Factors such as education, previous experience, type and size of employer, and geographic location influence compensation. Not surprisingly, paralegals who work for large law firms and those employed in major metropolitan areas tend to earn more than those who work for smaller firms or in less-populated regions.

In addition to a salary, many paralegals receive bonuses. Reports of total compensation usually include bonuses along with the regular salary.

According to the U.S. Department of Labor, full-time paralegals and legal assistants had median annual earnings, including bonuses, of $37,950 in 2002. The middle 50 percent earned between $30,020 and $48,760. The top 10 percent earned more than $61,150, while the bottom 10 percent earned less than $24,470. Median annual earnings in the industries employing the largest numbers of paralegals in 2002 were as follows:

Federal government	$53,770
Legal services	$36,780
Local government	$36,030
State government	$34,750

Specialty Areas

It is not uncommon to find salaries for paralegals and legal assistants varying significantly from one specialty area to another. According to the 2002 National Utilization and Compensation Survey study conducted by the National Association of Legal Assistants, total compensation by specialty ranged from $33,931 for those spending at least 40 percent of their time specializing in collections, to $50,076 for specialists focusing at least 40 percent of their time on legal matters related to aviation. The average total annual compensation in selected specialty areas was as follows:

Administrative/government/public	$42,753
Admiralty/maritime	$39,200
Aviation	$50,076

Banking/finance	$44,299
Bankruptcy	$39,222
Collections	$33,931
Contract	$45,746
Corporate	$48,648
Criminal	$38,221
Entertainment	$41,840
Environmental law	$43,758
Medical malpractice	$41,872
Personal injury	$39,996
Real estate	$45,496
Tax	$42,184
Telecommunications	$52,560

Geographical Differences

The 2002 survey by the National Association of Legal Assistants also revealed that geography played a major role in the range of salaries and bonuses earned by paralegals. In fact, average total annual compensation paid for the benchmark position of legal assistant/paralegal varied by nearly $18,000 over the seven reported regions. The average annual total compensation for this position by region was reported as follows:

Region 1: New England/East	$46,268
Region 2: Great Lakes	$41,500
Region 3: Plains States	$38,333
Region 4: Southeast	$42,429
Region 5: Southwest	$44,306
Region 6: Rocky Mountains	$37,667
Region 7: Far West	$55,068

Other Factors Affecting Compensation

In addition to factors such as the size and type of firm and the geographic location, other considerations can play an important part in salaries. Related job experience is understandably a major factor, and those who are just starting their careers may expect to earn less than those who have many years of experience. Similarly, paralegals working for nonprofit organizations, especially smaller ones, tend to earn less than those employed by corporations or private law firms.

Those who hold supervisory paralegal positions generally earn more than those without management responsibilities. Some paralegals with significant experience (usually at least three to five years) may be assigned to hire and supervise paralegals for an entire firm, or for a specialty area within a firm. Salary, in part, may depend on the paralegal's assertiveness and willingness to assume more work or more responsibility.

"When you are valuable, you have more bargaining power. It is only productive to be assertive if you are skilled at what you are doing," one paralegal advises. If you only do a minimal job, never ask questions, and never use independent judgment, you will not rise in the paralegal ranks.

As a paralegal, you will not become rich. However, it is important to see if you are being offered a fair starting salary. When judging a salary offer, be sure to see what fringe benefits are included. Also, see how often you can expect a raise and how this will be determined. In some firms, raises are automatic every six months. In other places, a raise depends on your supervisor's evaluation of your work and is based strictly on merit (as your supervisor sees it). Other firms and the federal government follow a salary schedule in determining raises. Some firms provide annual bonuses, based on the firm's profits for that year.

Many aspiring paralegals are uninformed about the salary levels available and want to start at the top of the salary scale. If such high salaries do come, they come only after at least five years of increasingly responsible work. Also, many of the first jobs a paralegal can obtain are tedious and border on drudgery. Many paralegals have little client contact and few meaningful strategy sessions with lawyers on a day-to-day basis.

Ambitious but patient paralegals may be willing to work for a large law firm documenting cases and doing other tedious work just to get the experience and have the name of a prestigious law firm on their résumés. Many of these firms are aware of this situation, and their salaries are lower.

Benefits

Salaries or wages are only part of the story when it comes to compensation. Many employers also provide their staff with various fringe benefits. Health insurance, retirement plans, and other benefits can add tremendously to the overall value of the compensation provided for working as a paralegal.

According to the National Association of Legal Assistants, about 74 percent of paralegals and legal assistants responding in a 2002 survey participated in a retirement or pension plan sponsored by the employer. Approximately 41 percent enjoyed a profit-sharing plan.

Other benefits, and the percentage of paralegals receiving them, included the following:

Health insurance	68 percent
Life insurance	63 percent
Dental insurance	40 percent
Disability insurance	50 percent

Free representation	41 percent
Maternity benefits	50 percent
Parking	62 percent
Child care	2 percent
Leased car	4 percent
Mileage	65 percent
Professional dues	77 percent
Health insurance for family	29 percent
Life insurance for family	29 percent

Not all employers provide the same kinds of benefits. Most of those who employ paralegals provide some, if not all, of the following:

- Holidays
- Sick time
- Vacation time
- Personal time
- General medical insurance
- Dental insurance
- Life insurance
- Travel/accident insurance
- Disability insurance
- Retirement plans
- Tuition assistance

When considering job opportunities, fringe benefits should be evaluated as a part of the overall compensation offered. In some cases, you might even consider taking a job with a lower salary than an equivalent job with another employer, if the benefits package is substantially better.

7

Pursuing Jobs

Searching for the right job can be a challenging process. But with the right combination of effort and good luck, you can find the ideal position for you.

The first step in trying to get a job is to assess the job situations in different geographic areas. The second step is to determine where you would like to work. The third step is to see how closely you can match the two.

Where Can You Find Paralegal Jobs?

Paralegal jobs can be found in a wide variety of areas. For starters, see how to obtain employment with your state and local area, municipality, township, or county. If they use a civil service registry, get on it. Then see what is available for those on the registry.

Some people get jobs in private law firms through their contacts; that is, one person knowing someone or knowing about a job somewhere. To pursue this approach, call people you know who are in influential positions, and ask them if they know of any openings for a person with your background. This is called networking.

When you are networking, the person with whom you speak may not understand what a paralegal is. Be prepared to explain it along with a brief description of what you personally can do. Do not say that you will accept whatever position is available. Give the person some examples. Perhaps you feel confident drafting pleadings in a law office, writing a newsletter involving legal issues, or tracking legislation. Emphasize your special skills. They may or may not be formally learned. For example, some untrained people may be better at negotiations than others who may have training but lack the temperament.

Call people who have jobs similar to the position you think you might want. Talk to them about their jobs. They will probably be flattered that you chose to talk to them, and they may know of openings for you to explore.

A more structured approach is to find paralegal jobs through Internet job sites, employer Web pages, classified ads, employment agencies, or the career services office at the school where you completed paralegal studies. The latter can be especially helpful if you take the time to get to know the staff and consult with them frequently when you are ready to seek employment.

Some local paralegal associations run job banks to help their members get jobs. For this help alone, it may pay to join a local paralegal association. Several national associations (see Appendix A) also offer job and career information, typically through their websites.

When talking to someone about a job, responding to online job postings, or answering a "help wanted" ad from the newspaper, you will need a résumé. Writing a résumé will take time. Be sure to style your résumé to meet the needs of the job you are seeking. You may wish to have two or three basic résumés ready to use, each with a different focus. Of course, each résumé is sent with a personal cover letter that addresses the specific qualifications the employer is seeking. If you are applying via e-mail or the Internet, a covering e-mail message or the electronic equivalent of a cover letter can still be helpful.

For example, Smith and Smith, Attorneys at Law, posts an ad on its website for a paralegal that says: "Legal assistant to research regulations on liquor laws and handle office reception in legal aid clinic."

Your reply should include mention of any research you have done in this or a similar area. Perhaps you wrote a term paper on the dangers of driving while intoxicated. You could explain that this gave you some familiarity with liquor laws. You also should explain that you enjoy meeting people and helping them resolve their problems. Since legal clinics depend on fast client turnover, you might mention that you work well under pressure and can turn out a finished product in a short time. However, do not make such statements unless they are true.

For many career-oriented paralegals, salary alone is not a decisive factor. Consideration should be given to the substance of the work and the scope of responsibility. In most cases, you will be working at your job from nine to five, so your work should be interesting.

The turnover rate for paralegals is quite high in both the public and private sectors. Some beginning paralegals will accept any job for the experience, regardless of the duties or the salary. If you do this, be sure you know when to leave the firm and set about looking for new and more challenging employment. In this field, it is not unusual for people to move around frequently. It does not look bad on your résumé to have been employed by two or three firms over a period of four or five years. However, be sure that your career planning involves learning new skills and increasing your salary with each change.

Working Conditions

Typically, paralegals complete most of their work at desks in offices and law libraries. Sometimes they may travel to gather information and perform other duties.

Those employed by corporations and government generally work a standard forty-hour week. Although most paralegals work year-round, some are temporarily employed during busy times of the year and then released when the workload diminishes. Paralegals who work for law firms sometimes work very long hours and are often under pressure to meet deadlines. Some law firms reward such loyalty with bonuses and additional time off.

Paralegals handle many routine assignments, particularly when they are inexperienced. Some find that these assignments offer little challenge, and they become frustrated with their duties. However, paralegals usually assume more responsible and varied tasks as they gain experience. Furthermore, as new laws and judicial interpretations emerge, paralegals are exposed to many new legal problems that make their work more interesting and challenging.

Atmosphere and Work Space

In considering possible places of employment, don't forget that the atmosphere of an office is important. Some offices are dreary places, every person going about his or her duty without time to smile or say hello. Other places, often more efficient ones, are run on a friendlier basis, with people doing some socializing. Look around you. Are people mumbling under their breath? Do they have personal effects such as pictures on their desks, or is the office a sterile place?

Although the general tenor of an office is important, so, too, is the specific area where you will be expected to do your work. Will you be given your own office? If not, will you have a partition around your desk? Is your desk in a high-traffic area so that you could easily be distracted by the noise and confusion around you?

The Procedural Angle

In fulfilling your duties, are there specific procedures you will be expected to follow? Did your predecessor leave a complete job description and form book for you to follow? If you are starting a new position without any of these items, will you be expected to develop your own forms and procedures? Are you up to this challenge, or do you prefer a more traditional approach?

Reporting and Evaluation

Obviously, you will not be performing your duties in a vacuum. With whom will you be working? Will you be on a team, and if so, are the members of the team compatible? How much responsibility will you be granted? Can you accept working under close supervision, or do you work better with minimal supervision?

To whom do you report? To another paralegal? To an attorney? Are there formal standards for evaluation of your work? How often will you be evaluated? Ask to see the criteria on which you will be evaluated so you know how best to prepare for your evaluation. Nothing is more frustrating than doing excellent work in one area and then not having it considered in your evaluation. Some supervisors are patient, helpful people; others are not. If you have a snappy, or even a nasty, supervisor, can you handle work under such pressure?

Professional Development

An important part of your career as a paralegal involves learning new things. Many private firms, as well as government and public sector law offices, offer in-house training in new areas, or support attendance at conferences or enrollment in college classes. Advancement may be based on your ability to handle new or additional duties. Will your employer allow you time to attend a course or seminar helpful to your work? Will the employer pay for the full cost of such training?

Work Schedule

Some people are early risers. Others cannot seem to get going until midafternoon. Do you have the opportunity to select your own hours so you can perform at your efficient best? Some government and private firms are allowing employees the opportunity to work within a "flextime" schedule, being on the job for thirty-five or forty hours per week but not necessarily from nine to five. Flextime usually extends from 7:00 A.M. to 7:00 P.M.

For people with family responsibilities, flextime can work well. In some cases, paralegal positions are only part-time. Some firms employ paralegals on a case-by-case basis. This is especially true in the areas of civil litigation and domestic relations.

Other Factors

Other practical considerations include how far your office is from your home. If you have to fight traffic for an hour or more each way, you might not be calm enough to handle all the demands of a paralegal position. A position that may pay less money but involves only a short drive may make more sense for you. When parking fees in some urban areas are up to $12 per day, parking your car may be a major consideration. Some employers provide free parking, and this benefit may be worth several hundred dollars per year for you.

Sometimes small things make a difference in your job satisfaction. Can you drink coffee at your desk? Surprisingly, many firms do not allow this. Does the office have a refrigerator or microwave for keeping or heating food? Many offices are located in areas near snack shops or grocery stores. This is helpful for a lunch break or a midafternoon snack.

Some firms or lawyers with whom you work may offer additional help. Some paralegals have their income taxes prepared free. Others have received some help with investments. Still others have obtained legal help in divorces or custody matters. Of course, many of these extra benefits depend on the relationship between the paralegal and the attorney.

Personal Aptitudes

Most paralegals enjoy their work. However, many warn would-be paralegals of some of the drawbacks of this field. Most paralegal work involves a great deal of pressure to get things done accurately and on time. In the public sector, a large caseload is an additional pressure; often several hundred cases are open at any one time.

Practicing paralegals use terms such as "meticulous" or "careful" to describe their work style. They suggest that would-be paralegals should feel comfortable with detail work.

Several practicing paralegals suggest that the prospective paralegal should have an inquiring mind, similar to that of an investigative reporter. Paralegals in many positions are given a problem and must figure out the best strategy to solve it.

For most paralegal positions, the individual should have the ability to use both written and spoken language well. One paralegal recommends that new members of the profession be good readers.

Women and Minorities

The majority of paralegals are women. However, there are also opportunities in this field for men. Some paralegals believe sexism is a declining problem in this field, especially in the larger, private firms. In smaller firms, there may still be a tendency for male lawyers to lump paralegals with the other "girls." Yet, this attitude is still a problem for some women attorneys as well. Opportunities are available, especially in private firms, for minorities.

Job Rating Checklist

Use the following job rating checklist as you evaluate prospective positions. Read through all the questions listed and mark a plus sign in the space provided at the far left if that factor is important to you. If not, leave the space blank. This will give you a picture of your "ideal" position.

Next, evaluate the specific position being considered, using the same criteria. This time, put a check mark in the second space at the left if the answer to the questions is "yes." If not, leave the space blank.

Now go back through the checklist and see how the prospective position measures up, point by point, to your ideal position. Remember that some factors should be weighted more heavily than others, depending on your personal circumstances. If the prospective position diverges greatly from the factors comprising your ideal job, you probably would not be happy in it.

Checklist
1. Job duties
   __ __ Are all your duties spelled out?
   __ __ Are they interesting and varied?
   __ Will you learn new things?
   __ __ Are form books available?
   __ __ Are you expected to do your own word processing and photocopying?
2. Salary
   __ __ Is the salary sufficient to meet your needs?
   __ __ Is there opportunity for a raise within six months? Within a year?
   __ __ Are you paid for overtime?
   __ __ Are you reimbursed for meals when you have to work late?
   __ __ Is there a yearly bonus?
3. Benefits
   __ __ Is health insurance provided?
   __ __ Is family coverage provided?
   __ __ Is pregnancy covered under health or disability plans?
   __ __ Is dental insurance provided?
   __ __ Is there a retirement plan paid for by the employer?
   __ __ Is personal leave granted? How much?
   __ __ Is child care a benefit option?

4. Supervision
— — Will your immediate supervisor be pleasant and fair?
— — Does your supervisor have the time and patience to explain new duties to you?
— — Will you be evaluated according to a set schedule and published criteria?

5. Coworkers
— — Do all members of the staff understand your status?
— — Do they respect it?
— — Is the office a friendly place with smiling people?

6. Training
— — Is in-house training provided?
— — Will employer pay for other training?
— — Will employer provide educational benefits?

7. Work space
— — Will you have your own office?
— — Will you be able to put pictures on the wall or place personal items on your desk?
— — Is your work space in a quiet area?

8. Work hours
— — Do your work hours fit your personal and/or family schedule?
— — Is flex time allowed?
— — Will your weekends be free?
— — Are part-time opportunities available?
— — Is vacation time with pay allowed the first year?

9. Transportation
— — Do you need a car to get to work?
— — Does it take you a long time to get to work?
— — Is parking provided free?

10. Amenities
— — Is the office clean?
— — Is there free coffee? Tea? Soft drinks?
— — Is there a place for heating food?
— — Is there a refrigerator?
— — Does the smoking policy meet your personal preferences?
— — Is there an inexpensive cafeteria or restaurant nearby?

11. Other items
— — Do you get legal help at a reduced rate?
— — Can you get help on your taxes either free or at a reduced rate?
— — (Add other considerations important to you here.)

Making Career Decisions

Career decisions are seldom easy. You may not be aware of all the options open to you. You may be uncertain of your chances of success, or whether a given set of job duties will be right for you. For reasons such as these, you should make every attempt to get all the facts before making your decision.

It is important to talk with others working in the field. You also should discuss career alternatives with your family, and perhaps with friends. Make sure, however, that the ultimate decision is yours.

Deciding on a career should be a positive experience. Remember, no career decision is irrevocable; you can always shift gears. In fact, most people have several careers during their working lives. Just be sure that you learn and grow in each position you take.

Leave the door open at all times for further advancement or, possibly, for a gracious exit.

Many women returning to the workforce do not know how to translate the skills they have acquired as homemakers into the skills required by employers. Some additional training and a good deal of courage may be all that is required. Employers of paralegals often prefer to hire women returning to the workforce because they are usually more mature and stable.

Retired or former military personnel also make excellent paralegals because they can bring their maturity and structured thinking to bear on complex legal or social problems.

Since a large portion of your time will be spent at your job, it is vital that you feel good about what you are doing. People who hate their jobs may feel so bad about what they do that they do not have the energy to seek other jobs. You can avoid this situation by realistically assessing your own needs and capabilities and then learning all you can about your chosen career field.

Good luck in your paralegal career. Remember, it is up to you to structure your position and your career. There are growing opportunities in the paralegal field, but there is also much competition for jobs. If you have found a position that meets your needs, you should look forward to a bright future in paralegal work.

8

Issues of Interest to Paralegals

One of the major issues in the paralegal profession involves the question of certification. Certification is the process of limiting the number of persons who desire to enter a profession to those who meet certain established standards.

More on Certification

Over the years, the issue of state certification has continued to come up. Certification requirements were once in effect in Oregon, but they were abolished because very few paralegals bothered to become certified. Over the past few decades, certification legislation has been considered in a number of states including California, Michigan, Wyoming, and North Carolina. State bar associations that have considered certification include California, Kansas, Illinois, Mississippi, Missouri, and South Dakota.

In several states, the bar initially was in favor of regulating paralegal activity directly. Most paralegal groups objected; they fought for regulation of paralegals by paralegals. Consequently, instead of regulating paralegals directly, the bar associations have established guidelines for attorneys that elaborate on the existing Code of Professional Responsibility. The American Bar Association (ABA) has put forth the following guidelines for the use of legal assistants by attorneys:

1. A lawyer is responsible for all of the professional actions of a legal assistant performing legal assistant services at the lawyer's direction and should take reasonable measures to ensure that the legal assistant's conduct is consistent with the lawyer's obligations under the ABA Model Rules of Professional Conduct.

2. Provided the lawyer maintains responsibility for the work product, a lawyer may delegate to a legal assistant any task normally performed by the lawyer except those tasks proscribed to one not licensed as a lawyer by statute, court rule, administrative rule or regulation, controlling authority, the ABA Model Rules of Professional Conduct, or these Guidelines.

3. A lawyer may not delegate to a legal assistant:

   a. Responsibility for establishing an attorney-client relationship.
   b. Responsibility for establishing the amount of a fee to be charged for a legal service.
   c. Responsibility for a legal opinion rendered to a client.

4. It is the lawyer's responsibility to take reasonable measures to ensure that clients, courts, and other lawyers are aware that a legal assistant, whose services are utilized by the lawyer in performing legal services, is not licensed to practice law.

5. A lawyer may identify legal assistant by name and title on the lawyer's letterhead and on business cards identifying the lawyer's firm.

6. It is the responsibility of a lawyer to take reasonable measures to ensure that all client confidences are preserved by the legal assistant.

7. A lawyer should take reasonable measures to prevent conflicts of interest resulting from a legal assistant's other employment of interests insofar as such other employment or interest would present a conflict of interest if it were that of the lawyer.

8. A lawyer may include a charge for the work performed by a legal assistant in setting a charge for legal services.

9. A lawyer may not split legal fees with a legal assistant nor pay a legal assistant for the referral of legal business. A lawyer may compensate a legal assistant based on the quantity of the legal assistant's work and the value of that work to a law practice, but the legal assistant's compensation may not be contingent, by advance agreement, upon the profitability of the lawyer's practice.

10. A lawyer who employs a legal assistant should facilitate the legal assistant's participation in appropriate continuing education and in pro bono public activities.

How Paralegals View Certification

Many paralegals believe that such guidelines or regulations by bar associations should be discouraged. At the same time, several professional organizations offer their own certification programs. These include the National Association of Legal Assistants (nala.org), the National Federation of Paralegal Associations (paralegals.org), and NALS, the association for legal professionals (formerly known as the National Association of Legal Secretaries, but now known simply as NALS). In 2004 the latter organization established the Certified PP (Professional Paralegal) designation for paralegals who wish to be identified as exceptional in all areas of law. The certificate is awarded to paralegals who pass a one-day, four-part examination.

According to NALS, successful completion of this exam demonstrates:

- A mastery of procedural skills and communication skills
- An advanced knowledge of procedural law, the law library, and the preparation of legal documents
- A working knowledge of substantive law and the ability to perform specifically delegated substantive legal work under an attorney's supervision
- The ability to interact on a professional level with attorneys, clients, and other staff
- The discipline to assume responsibility and exercise initiative and judgment while adhering to legal ethical standards at all times

Working under the supervision of a practicing lawyer or a judge, the Certified PP is expected to possess:

- The same high standard of ethical conduct imposed upon members of the bar
- Excellent written and verbal communication skills
- Knowledge and understanding of legal terminology and procedures, as well as procedural and substantive law
- The ability to assume responsibility, exercise initiative and judgment, and prepare substantive legal documents within the scope of assigned authority

Attaining this goal demonstrates dedication to professionalism and acceptance of the challenge to be exceptional. Personal motivation is necessary to attain such a goal.

To be eligible to take the exam, an applicant must have five years of experience performing paralegal/legal assistant duties, or a specified combination of experience and paralegal education. Topics covered by the exam include written communications, legal knowledge and skills, ethics and judgment skills, and substantive law.

A number of state and local chapters of NALS sponsor a course for preparing for the exam. For more details, contact a chapter in your area, or consult the national offices at the following address:

NALS Resource Center
314 East Third Street, Suite 210
Tulsa, Oklahoma 74120
nals.org

Everyone doesn't agree about the value of certification, or that it should be required. Some argue that paralegals are being used in ways people never contemplated earlier and that experimentation in the use of paralegals is growing. They fear that premature certification will curtail this experimentation and thus limit opportunities for paralegals.

In addition, certification might restrict the field to those who have graduated from specific schools, thus limiting the individual's freedom to choose the training route best suited to him or her. Some paralegals specialize in one field and are not competent in other legal areas. Certification might rule out their standing as paralegals, no matter how qualified they are in their particular fields.

Some are concerned that certification also might impair those paralegals who learned their skills on the job rather than through a formal training program. Under this thinking, paralegals who are former legal secretaries would become second-class paralegals if certification were required.

As it now stands, certification is voluntary. Many paralegals hope it will stay that way.

Ethics and Responsibilities

In addition to the issue of certification, the National Association of Legal Assistants believes that paralegals should adhere to specific rules of conduct in their profession.

Their canons of conduct are as follows:

- **Canon 1.** A legal assistant shall not perform any of the duties that lawyers only may perform nor do things that lawyers themselves may not do.
- **Canon 2.** A legal assistant may perform any task delegated and supervised by a lawyer so long as the lawyer is responsible to the client, maintains a direct relationship with the client, and assumes full professional responsibility for the work product.
- **Canon 3.** A legal assistant shall not engage in the practice of law by giving legal advice, appearing in court, setting fees, or accepting cases.
- **Canon 4.** A legal assistant shall not act in matters involving professional legal judgment as the services of a lawyer are essential in the public interest whenever the exercise of such judgment is required.
- **Canon 5.** A legal assistant must act prudently in determining the extent to which a client may be assisted without the presence of a lawyer.

- **Canon 6.** A legal assistant shall not engage in the unauthorized practice of law and shall assist in preventing the unauthorized practice of law.

- **Canon 7.** A legal assistant must protect the confidences of a client, and it shall be unethical for a legal assistant to violate any statute now in effect or hereafter to be enacted controlling privileged communications.

- **Canon 8.** It is the obligation of the legal assistant to avoid conduct which would cause the lawyer to be unethical or even appear to be unethical, and loyalty to the employer is incumbent upon the legal assistant.

- **Canon 9.** A legal assistant shall work continually to maintain integrity and a high degree of competency throughout the legal profession.

- **Canon 10.** A legal assistant shall strive for perfection through education in order to better assist the legal profession in fulfilling its duty of making legal services available to clients and the public.

- **Canon 11.** A legal assistant shall do all other things incidental, necessary, or expedient for the attainment of the ethics and responsibilities imposed by statute or rule of court.

- **Canon 12.** A legal assistant is governed by the American Bar Association Code of Professional Responsibility.

9

RELATED CAREERS IN THE COURTS

LAWYERS ARE FAR from the only workers employed in our court system. A variety of "nonlawyers" also hold various positions in court. Some of these jobs are paralegal in nature, others are "parajudicial," that is, employing judges who are not lawyers. This chapter provides a brief look at a variety of careers and jobs in the courts for nonlawyers.

Court Administrators

Many twenty-first-century courts are managed by professional court administrators. Several schools offer training programs for court administrators. They cover topics such as evaluating and maintaining the organization, practices, and procedures of courts; keeping records and compiling data; planning and monitoring the allocation of resources; managing court personnel systems; and designing, implementing, and operating management systems.

Probation, marital support, mental health, and juvenile cases are all examples of administrative or managerial functions arising from judicial decisions. Many of these issues are now handled by court administrators.

A nationwide survey of law enforcement criminal justice needs and resources revealed that the need for professional court managers who are trained in management skills will increase as court caseloads increase. Reorganizations are eliminating smaller courts (justice of the peace courts) and creating a need for individuals—possibly paralegal personnel—to handle minor cases, according to respected authorities in the field.

Some of the specific duties that court administrators can assume include better scheduling of jurors' time and more efficient notification of trial cancellations through greater use of computers. Some court administrators have prepared budgets that allow for minor court remodeling that will make the courts more accessible for persons with disabilities. Other responsibilities include personnel management—seeing to the needs of the professional and nonprofessional court workers. Such court workers include judges, parajudges, lawyers, paralegals, law enforcement officers, social workers, interpreters, budget experts, court reporters, secretaries, clerks, and maintenance crews.

The court administrator may be in charge of preparing a budget for the fiscal year and then lobbying the legislature to get the budget passed. The court administrator also might be in charge of the physical condition of the court—seeing to it that appropriate artwork is purchased or that the grounds are kept clean. Although court administrators would not do all these tasks themselves, they would be in charge of seeing that they got done.

Other upper administrative management positions include federal court circuit executive, clerk of court, jury commissioner, and chief probation officer. These positions involve highly responsible administrative and supervisory work.

A bachelor's degree, and preferably a master's degree, in public or business administration, legal administration, or a related field is required.

Other Professional Positions

In addition to administrative positions in the court, there are other nonlegal professional positions. These include management specialists, budget and fiscal analysts, accountants and auditors, employee and judicial training specialists, law librarians, interpreters, statisticians, and researchers.

Requirements for professional staff members and their compensation vary with each jurisdiction. Generally, these positions require a college degree and some specialized training or experience.

Those interested in working in any of the U.S. courts should address their letters or e-mails and résumés to the clerk of the court in the jurisdiction where they wish to work. Each court does its own recruiting, hiring, and firing.

Counselors and Social Workers

Courts also use the services of counselors and social workers. Traditionally, courts have employed probation and parole officials to handle counseling. Now, courts are expanding these services and require additional personnel. Other courts also employ psychologists and youth workers.

Generally, these social service positions require a bachelor's degree. Most probation departments offer in-house training programs. Federal probation officers must hold a graduate degree in social work, psychology, criminal justice, criminology, or a related field. Many of these positions are filled through the civil service system.

Modern courts often use court specialists who must know how to operate a variety of computer systems. Thus, anyone interested in court management must be computer literate and have knowledge of current software and hardware.

Clerical Positions

The majority of positions in the courts are technical, clerical, or secretarial. Persons who assist judges in handling the massive amount of paperwork often are called deputy clerks. These deputy clerks advise the public, paralegals, or attorneys about court rules on form and procedure. People who work in the courts at this level should be individuals who enjoy keeping things in order. Court secretaries and stenographers are used extensively by judges. These individuals generally have secretarial experience and are able to follow directions and work with great accuracy.

Clerks of the Court

Most courts have a clerk of the court, generally a paralegal position. In some jurisdictions, however, this role is restricted to lawyers. The following sampling of state clerks of the court will give you a good idea of the duties and responsibilities involved.

• In Alabama, the chief clerk of the probate court administers oaths and receives documents and proofs of instruments for certification. When there is no contest involved, the chief clerk exercises all the power and authority of the probate judge.

- In Arkansas, the clerk of the county court is elected. This individual attends each session of the court and keeps an accurate record of its proceedings. The clerk also keeps a regular account of the county treasury and files and preserves papers dealing with the settlements of any accounts involving the county.

- In California, the clerk of the municipal court keeps minutes and other records of the courts. The clerk may appoint deputies.

- In Colorado, the clerks of the county court keep both judicial and financial records.

- In Delaware, the clerks of the court of common pleas take care of the records and proceedings of the court. The clerk receives and pays all fines, fees, and costs. In addition, the clerk administers oaths and issues commitments and executions. The clerk is appointed by judges and holds office at their pleasure. The clerks of family court in this state take care of legal records and collect fees, fines, costs, and bail. They also may issue summonses and warrants. They are appointed by the chief judge.

- In Maryland, the chief administrative clerk of the district court is appointed by the chief judge. This individual is charged with the maintenance and operation of clerical staff and the district's workload. This includes supervision of dockets, records, and other necessary papers.

- In Texas, the clerk of the county court is elected to a four-year term. The clerk's duties include issuing marriage licenses, administering oaths, taking depositions, and acting as county recorder and keeper of court records. The clerk may appoint deputies.

- In Hawaii, the land court registrar attends sessions of court, keeps a docket of all cases, and seals all papers and processes. This person has custody of all documents, administers oaths, and receives fees. Similar duties are accorded the registrar of probate in Maine and the land court recorder in Massachusetts.

Court Reporters

Court reporters are another group vital to the functioning of the courts. Court reporters record trial proceedings verbatim through the use of shorthand, special typewriters (stenotype machines), or tape recorders. In most places court reporters are in short supply and command high salaries, generally quite a bit higher than the average paralegal. Some states require certification of court reporters and proof of U.S. citizenship prior to employment.

Many schools offer programs in court reporting, often as part of an associate degree or certificate.

Security Officials

Various courts employ law enforcement officials called bailiffs, sheriffs, and marshals. They transport prisoners, serve court orders and writs, and maintain order in the courtroom. These positions generally require graduation from high school. They are often filled through the state's civil service commission.

While security positions have long been a necessary part of the court system, they have taken on an additional aura of importance in the post–September 11 era.

Parajudges

Another group of court workers are parajudges. They are appointed by the court to assist in judicial decision making. Most, but not all, are lawyers. Parajudges hold hearings, determine facts, and make recommendations, but they may not enter final judgments. Common parajudicial titles include referee, magistrate, commissioner, master, and hearing officer.

Check-Out Receipt

Alameda Free Library
Main Branch
1550 Oak Street
Alameda, CA
Tel: 510-747-7777
www.alamedafree.org

Checkout Date: 05-23-2015 - 15:10:01

Patron ID.: xxxxxxxxxx4968

---

1 The paralegal /
33341000567528   Due Date: 06/13/15
2 Finding me : a decade of darkne
33341007815318   Due Date: 06/13/15

---

otal Items: 2

Balance Due: $ 4.00

Check us out on social media!
Twitter: @alamedafree
acebook: facebook.com/alamedafreelibrary

Check-Out Receipt

Alameda Free Library
Main Branch
1550 Oak Street
Alameda, CA
Tel: 510-747-7777
www.alamedafree.org

Checkout Date: 05-23-2015 - 15:10:01

Patron ID.: xxxxxxxxxxxx4568

---

1 The paralegal /
33341005945326   Due Date: 06/13/15
2 Finding me : a decade of darkne
33341007945318   Due Date: 06/13/15

Total Items: 2

Balance Due: $ 4.00

Check us out on social media!
Twitter: @alamedafree
Facebook: facebook.com/alamedafreelibrary

APPENDIX A

National Associations

American Association of Law Libraries
53 W. Jackson Blvd., Ste. 940
Chicago, IL 60604
aallnet.org

American Association for Paralegal Education
407 Wekiva Springs Rd., Ste. 241
Longwood, FL 32779
aafpe.org

American Bar Association
Standing Committee on Paralegals
321 N. Clark St.
Chicago, IL 60610
abanet.org/legalservices/legalassistants

Association of Legal Administrators
75 Tri-State International, Ste. 222
Lincolnshire, IL 60069
alanet.org

Canadian Association of Paralegals
Postal Box 967, Station "B"
Montréal, Québec
Canada H3B 3K5
caplegal.ca

Legal Assistant Management Association
P.O. Box 659
Avondale Estates, GA 30002
lamanet.org

National Association of Legal Assistants
1516 Boston Ave., Ste. 200
Tulsa, OK 74119
nala.org

National Federation of Paralegal Associations
2517 Eastlake Ave. East, Ste. 200
Seattle, WA 98102
paralegals.org

Appendix B

Legal Periodicals

The Journal of Paralegal Education and Practice
American Association for Paralegal Education
407 Wekiva Springs Rd., Ste. 241
Longwood, FL 32779
aafpe.org

Legal Assistant Today
James Publishing
P.O. Box 25202
Santa Ana, CA 92799
legalassistanttoday.com

National Paralegal Reporter
National Federation of Paralegal Associations
2517 Eastlake Ave. East, Ste. 200
Seattle, WA 98102
paralegals.org

The Paralegal Educator
American Association for Paralegal Education
407 Wekiva Springs Rd., Ste. 241
Longwood, FL 32779
aafpe.org
(quarterly)

The Practical Lawyer
ALI-ABA
4025 Chestnut St.
Philadelphia, PA 19104
ali-aba.org
(six times per year)

Schools Offering Paralegal Training Programs

The following list is arranged alphabetically. It does not include all schools, but it does provide a representative sampling. Check with the higher education agency in your state or province for more details.

Alabama

Auburn University at Montgomery
Montgomery, AL 36124
aum.edu

Faulkner University
Montgomery, AL 36109
faulkner.edu

Gadsden State Community College
Gadsden, AL 35902
gadsdenst.cc.al.us

Northeast Alabama Community College
Rainsville, AL 35986
nacc.edu

Samford University
Birmingham, AL 35229
samford.edu

South University
Montgomery, AL 36116
southuniversity.edu

Virginia College at Birmingham
Birmingham, AL 35219
vc.edu

Wallace State Community College
Hanceville, AL 35077
wallacestate.edu

Alaska

University of Alaska, Anchorage
Anchorage, AK 99508
uaa.alaska.edu

University of Alaska, Fairbanks
Fairbanks, AK 99701
uaf.edu

University of Alaska, Southeast
Juneau, AK 99801
uas.alaska.edu

Arizona

Everest College
Phoenix, AZ 85021
cci.edu

Lamson College
Tempe, AZ 85281
lamsoncollege.com

Mohave Community College
Kingman, AZ 86401
mohave.edu

Phoenix Career College
Phoenix, AZ 85003
phoenixcareercollege.com

Phoenix College
Phoenix, AZ 85013
maricopa.edu

Pima Community College
Tucson, AZ 85709
pimacc.pima.edu

Yavapai College
Prescott, AZ 86301
yc.edu

Arkansas

University of Arkansas, Fort Smith
Fort Smith, AR 72913
uafortsmith.edu

British Columbia

Capilano College
North Vancouver, B.C.
Canada V7J 3H5
capcollege.bc.ca

California

California Polytechnic State University
San Luis Obispo, CA 93407
calpoly.edu

California State University, Hayward
Hayward, CA 94542
csuhayward.edu

California State University, Los Angeles
Los Angeles, CA 90032
calstatela.edu

Cerritos Community College
Norwalk, CA 90650
cerritos.edu

City College of San Francisco
San Francisco, CA 94112
ccsf.edu

Coastline Community College
Fountain Valley, CA 92708
cccd.edu

College of the Sequoias
Visalia, CA 93277
cos.edu

Cuyamaca Community College
El Cajon, CA 92019
gcccd.net

De Anza College
Cupertino, CA 95014
fhda.edu

El Camino College
Torrance, CA 90506
elcamino.edu

Fresno City College
Fresno, CA 93741
fresnocitycollege.com

Los Angeles City College
Los Angeles, CA 90029
lacitycollege.edu

Los Angeles Mission College
Sylmar, CA 91342
lamission.cc.ca.us

Mt. San Antonio College
Walnut, CA 91789
mtsac.edu

Palomar College
San Marcos, CA 92069
palomar.edu

Platt College
Cerritos, CA 90703
plattesu.com

Platt College
Ontario, CA 91764
plattcollege.com

Saint Mary's College
Moraga, CA 94575
stmarys-ca.edu

San Francisco State University
San Francisco, CA 94105
sfsu.edu

San Joaquin College of Law
Clovis, CA 93612
sjcl.edu

Santa Ana College
Santa Ana, CA 92706
sac.edu

Sonoma State University
Rohnert Park, CA 94928
sonoma.edu

Southwestern College
Chula Vista, CA 91910
swc.cc.ca.us

University of California, Irvine
Irvine, CA 92716
uci.edu

University of California, Los Angeles Extension
Los Angeles, CA 90024-2883
uclaextension.org

University of California, San Diego
UCSD Extension
San Diego, CA 92093
ucsd.edu

University of California, Santa Barbara Extension
Goleta, CA 93117
extension.ucsb.edu

University of La Verne
La Verne, CA 91750
ulv.edu

University of San Diego
San Diego, CA 92110
sandiego.edu

West Valley College
Saratoga, CA 95070
wvmccd.cc.ca.us

Colorado

Arapahoe Community College
Littleton, CO 80160
arapahoe.edu

Community College of Aurora
Aurora, CO 80011
ccaurora.edu

Pikes Peak Community College
Colorado Springs, CO 80903
ppcc.edu

Connecticut

Briarwood College
Southington, CT 06489
briarwood.edu

Hartford College for Women
Hartford, CT 06105
hartford.edu

Manchester Community College
Manchester, CT 06045
mcc.commnet.edu

Naugatuck Valley Community Technical College
Waterbury, CT 06708
commnet.edu

Quinnipiac University
Hamden, CT 06518
quinnipiac.edu

University of New Haven
West Haven, CT 06516
newhaven.edu

Delaware

Wesley College
Dover, DE 19901
wesley.edu

Widener University
Wilmington, DE 19803
widener.edu

District of Columbia

Georgetown University
Washington, DC 20057
georgetown.edu

Florida

Barry University
Miami Shores, FL 33161
barry.edu

Broward Community College
Hollywood, FL 33024
broward.edu

Edison Community College
Fort Myers, FL 33906
edison.edu

Florida Community College at Jacksonville
Jacksonville, FL 32205
fccj.edu

Florida Gulf Coast University
Fort Myers, FL 33965-6565
fgcu.edu

Florida International University
Miami, FL 33199
fiu.edu

Hillsborough Community College
Tampa, FL 33605
hhcc.cc.fl.us

Manatee Community College
Bradenton, FL 34209
mcc.cc.fl.us

Miami-Dade College
Miami, FL 33132
mdcc.edu

Nova Southeastern University
Fort Lauderdale, FL 33314
nova.edu

Palm Beach Community College
West Palm Beach, FL 33410
pbcc.edu

Pensacola Junior College
Pensacola, FL 32501
pjc.cc.fl.us

Santa Fe Community College
Gainesville, FL 32605
santafe.cc.fl.us

Seminole Community College
Sanford, FL 32773
scc-fl.com

University of Central Florida
Orlando, FL 32816
ucf.edu

University of North Florida
Jacksonville, FL 32224
unf.edu

University of West Florida
Pensacola, FL 32514
uwf.edu

Valencia Community College
Orlando, FL 32802
valencia.cc.fl.us

Georgia

Athens Technical College
Athens, GA 30601
aati.edu

Brenau University
Gainesville, GA 30501
brenau.edu

Clayton College & State University
Morrow, GA 30260
clayton.edu

Gainesville College
Gainesville, GA 30503
gc.peachnet.edu

South University
Savannah, GA 31406
southuniversity.edu

Hawaii

Kapi'olani Community College
Honolulu, HI 96816
hawaii.edu

Idaho

Boise State University
Boise, ID 83725
boisestate.edu

Eastern Idaho Technical College
Idaho Falls, ID 83404
eitc.edu

Idaho State University
Pocatello, ID 83209
isu.edu

Illinois

Elgin Community College
Elgin, IL 60123
elgin.edu

Illinois Central College
Peoria, IL 61635
icc.cc.il.us

Illinois State University
Normal, IL 61790
ilstu.edu

Kankakee Community College
Kankakee, IL 60901
kankakee.edu

Loyola University Chicago
Chicago, IL 60611
luc.edu

MacCormac College
Chicago, IL 60605-1667
maccormac.edu

Rockford Business College
Rockford, IL 61103
rbcsuccess.com

Roosevelt University
Chicago, IL 60605
roosevelt.edu

South Suburban College
South Holland, IL 60473
southsuburbancollege.edu

Southern Illinois University
Carbondale, IL 62901
siu.edu

Southwestern Illinois College
Belleville, IL 62221
southwestern.cc.il.us

William Rainey Harper College
Palatine, IL 60067
harper.cc.il.us

Indiana

Ball State University
Muncie, IN 47306
bsu.edu

Calumet College of St. Joseph
Whiting, IN 46394
ccsj.edu

Indiana University–Purdue University, Indianapolis
Indianapolis, IN 46202
iupui.edu

Indiana University, South Bend
South Bend, IN 46634-7111
iusb.edu

Ivy Tech State College
Fort Wayne, IN 46805
ivytech.edu

Ivy Tech State College, Region 6
Muncie, IN 47302
ivytech.edu

Saint Mary-of-the-Woods College
Saint Mary of the Woods, IN 47876
smwc.edu

University of Evansville
Evansville, IN 47722
evansville.edu

Vincennes University
Vincennes, IN 47591
indian.vinu.edu

Iowa

Des Moines Area Community College
Des Moines, IA 50314
dmacc.cc.ia.us

Kirkwood Community College
Cedar Rapids, IA 52406
kirkwood.cc.ia.us

Kansas

Johnson County Community College
Overland Park, KS 66210
jccc.net

Northwest Kansas Technical College
Atchison, KS 66002
nwktc.org

Washburn University
Topeka, KS 66621
washburn.edu

Kentucky

Beckfield College
Florence, KY 41022
beckfieldcollege.com

Daymar College
Owensboro, KY 42301
daymarcollege.com

Eastern Kentucky University
Richmond, KY 40475-3122
eku.edu

Morehead State University
Morehead, KY 40351
morehead-st.edu

Sullivan University
Louisville, KY 40205
sullivan.edu

Sullivan University, Lexington Campus
Lexington, KY 40504
sullivan.edu

University of Louisville
Louisville, KY 40292
louisville.edu

Louisiana

Herzing College
Kenner, LA 70062
herzing.edu

Louisiana State University
Baton Rouge, LA 70803-1530
lsu.edu

Tulane University
New Orleans, LA 70118
tulane.edu

University of New Orleans
New Orleans, LA 70130
uno.edu

Maine

Andover College
Portland, ME 04103
andovercollege.com

University of Maine, Augusta
Bangor, ME 04401
maine.edu

Maryland

Anne Arundel Community College
Arnold, MD 21012
aacc.cc.md.us

Community College of Baltimore County
Baltimore, MD 21222
ccbc.cc.md.us

Frederick Community College
Frederick, MD 21702
frederick.edu

Harford Community College
Bel Air, MD 21015
harford.edu

University of Maryland University College
Adelphi, MD 20783
umuc.edu

Villa Julie College
Stevenson, MD 21153
vjc.edu

Massachusetts

Anna Maria College
Paxton, MA 01612
annamaria.edu

Bay Path College
Longmeadow, MA 01106
baypath.edu

Elms College
Chicopee, MA 01013
elms.edu

North Shore Community College
Danvers, MA 01923
northshore.edu

Northeastern University
Boston, MA 02115
northeastern.edu

Northern Essex Community College
Haverhill, MA 01830
necc.mass.edu

Suffolk University
Boston, MA 02114
suffolk.edu

Michigan

Davenport University
Kalamazoo, MI 49006
davenport.edu

Davenport University, Grand Rapids
Grand Rapids, MI 49503
davenport.edu

Delta College
University Center, MI 48710
delta.edu

Eastern Michigan University
Ypsilanti, MI 48197
emich.edu

Ferris State University
Big Rapids, MI 49307
ferris.edu

Grand Valley State University
Grand Rapids, MI 49504
gvsu.edu

Henry Ford Community College
Dearborn, MI 48128
henryford.cc.mi.us

Kellogg Community College
Battle Creek, MI 49017
kellogg.edu

Lake Superior State University
Sault Ste. Marie, MI 49783
lssu.edu

Lansing Community College
Lansing, MI 48901
lcc.edu

Macomb Community College
Warren, MI 48088
macomb.edu

Madonna University
Livonia, MI 48150
madonna.edu

Northwestern Michigan College
Traverse City, MI 49686
nmc.edu

Oakland Community College
Farmington Hills, MI 48334
occ.cc.mi.us

Oakland University
Rochester, MI 48309
oakland.edu

Minnesota

Hamline University
Saint Paul, MN 55104
hamline.edu

Inver Hills Community College
Inver Grove Heights, MN 55076
inverhills.mnscu.edu

Minnesota Paralegal Institute
Minnetonka, MN 55305
mnparalegal.com

Minnesota School of Business/Globe College
Brooklyn Center, MN 55430
msbcollege.edu

Minnesota State University Moorhead
Moorhead, MN 56563
mnstate.edu

North Hennepin Community College
Brooklyn Park, MN 55445
nhcc.mnscu.edu

North Hennepin Community College
Minneapolis, MN 55445
nhcc.mnscu.edu

Winona State University
Winona, MN 55987
winona.msus.edu

Mississippi

Mississippi College
Clinton, MS 39058
mc.edu

Mississippi University for Women
Columbus, MS 39701
muw.edu

University of Mississippi
University, MS 38677
olemiss.edu

University of Southern Mississippi
Hattiesburg, MS 39406
usm.edu

Missouri

Avila University
Kansas City, MO 64145
avila.edu

Hickey College
Saint Louis, MO 63146
hickeycollege.edu

Maryville University
Saint Louis, MO 63141
maryville.edu

Missouri Western State College
St. Joseph, MO 64507
mwsc.edu

Penn Valley Community College
Kansas City, MO 64111
kcmetro.edu

Rockhurst College
Kansas City, MO 64110
rockhurst.edu

St. Louis Community College, Florissant Valley
St. Louis, MO 63135
stlcc.cc.mo.us

St. Louis Community College, Meramec
St. Louis, MO 63122
stlcc.edu

Webster University
St. Louis, MO 63119
webster.edu

William Woods University
Fulton, MO 65251
williamwoods.edu

Montana

University of Montana
Missoula, MT 59801
umt.edu

Nebraska

Central Community College
Grand Island, NE 68802
cccneb.edu

College of Saint Mary
Omaha, NE 68124
csm.edu

Metropolitan Community College
Omaha, NE 68103
mccneb.edu

Nevada

Community College of Southern Nevada
Las Vegas, NV 89146
ccsn.edu

New Hampshire

Hesser College
Manchester, NH 03103
hesser.edu

McIntosh College
Dover, NH 03820
mcintoshcollege.com

New Jersey

Atlantic Cape Community College
Mays Landing, NJ 08330
atlantic.edu

Bergen Community College
Paramus, NJ 07652
bergen.edu

Berkeley College
West Paterson, NJ 07424
berkeleycollege.edu

Brookdale Community College
Lincroft, NJ 07738
brookdalecc.edu

Burlington County College
Mount Laurel, NJ 08054
bcc.edu

Cumberland County College
Vineland, NJ 08362
cccnj.edu

Essex County Community College
Newark, NJ 07102
essex.edu

Fairleigh Dickinson University
Madison, NJ 07940
fdu.edu

Gloucester County College
Sewell, NJ 08619
gccnj.edu

Mercer County Community College
Trenton, NJ 08690
mccc.edu

Middlesex County College
Edison, NJ 08818
middlesexcc.edu

Montclair State University
Upper Montclair, NJ 07043
montclair.edu

Ocean County College
Toms River, NJ 08754
ocean.edu

Raritan Valley Community College
Somerville, NJ 08876
raritanval.edu

Warren County Community College
Washington, NJ 07882-4343
warren.edu

New Mexico

Albuquerque Technical Vocational Institute
Albuquerque, NM 87106
http://tvi.cc.nm.us

Dona Ana Branch Community College
Las Cruces, NM 88003
nmsu.edu

New Mexico State University, Alamogordo
Alamogordo, NM 88310
nmsu.edu

New York

Berkeley College
White Plains, NY 10601
berkeleycollege.edu

Bronx Community College
Bronx, NY 10453
bcc.cuny.edu

Corning Community College
Corning, NY 14830
corning-cc.edu

Dutchess Community College
Poughkeepsie, NY 12601
sunydutchess.edu

Erie Community College
Buffalo, NY 14203
ecc.edu

Fingerlakes Community College
Canandaigua, NY 14424
flcc.edu

Genesee Community College
Batavia, NY 14020
genesee.edu

Hilbert College
Hamburg, NY 14075
hilbert.edu

Hofstra University
Hempstead, NY 11549
hofstra.edu

LaGuardia Community College
Long Island City, NY 11101
lagcc.cuny.edu

Lehman College
Bronx, NY 10468
lehman.cuny.edu

Long Island University
Brooklyn, NY 11201
liu.edu

Marist College
Fishkill, NY 12524
marist.edu

Mercy College
Dobbs Ferry, NY 10522
mercy.edu

Monroe Community College
Rochester, NY 14604
monroecc.edu

Nassau Community College
Garden City, NY 11530
ncc.edu

New York City College of Technology
Brooklyn, NY 11201
citytech.cuny.edu

New York University
New York, NY 10007
nyu.edu

Queens College
Flushing, NY 11367
qc.edu

Rockland Community College
Suffern, NY 10901
sunyrockland.edu

Sage Colleges
Albany, NY 12208
sage.edu

Schenectady County Community College
Schenectady, NY 12305
sunysccc.edu

St. John's University
Jamaica, NY 11439
stjohns.edu

Suffolk County Community College
Selden, NY 11784
sunysuffolk.edu

SUNY/Westchester Community College
Valhalla, NY 10595-1698
sunywcc.edu

Syracuse University
Syracuse, NY 13244-2530
syr.edu

Tompkins Cortland Community College
Dryden, NY 13053
sunytccc.edu

North Carolina

Carteret Community College
Morehead City, NC 28557
carteret.edu

Central Piedmont Community College
Charlotte, NC 28235
cpcc.edu

Fayetteville Technical Community College
Fayetteville, NC 28303
faytecbcc.edu

Meredith College
Raleigh, NC 27607-5298
meredith.edu

Pitt Community College
Greenville, NC 27835
pitt.cc.nc.us

South Piedmont Community College
Monroe, NC 28110
southpiedmont.org

Western Piedmont Community College
Morganton, NC 28655
wp.cc.nc.us

North Dakota

Lake Region State College
Devils Lake, ND 58301
lrsc.nodak.edu

Ohio

Capital University Law School
Columbus, OH 43215
capital.edu

College of Mount St. Joseph
Cincinnati, OH 45233
msj.edu

Columbus State Community College
Columbus, OH 43215
cscc.edu

Cuyahoga Community College
Parma, OH 44130
tri-c.edu

Edison Community College
Piqua, OH 45356
edison.cc.oh.us

EHOVE Career Center
Milan, OH 44846
ehove-jvs.k12.oh.us

Kent State University
Kent, OH 44242
kent.edu

Kent State University, East Liverpool
East Liverpool, OH 43920
kenteliv.kent.edu

Lake Erie College
Painesville, OH 44077
lec.edu

Lakeland Community College
Willoughby, OH 44094
lakeland.cc.oh.us

Muskingum Area Technical College
Zanesville, OH 43701
matc.tec.oh.us

Myers University
Cleveland, OH 44115
myers.edu

North Central State College
Mansfield, OH 44901
ncstatecollege.edu

Shawnee State University
Portsmouth, OH 45662
shawnee.edu

Sinclair Community College
Dayton, OH 45402
sinclair.edu

University of Akron
Akron, OH 44325
uakron.edu

University of Cincinnati, Clermont
Batavia, OH 45103
uc.edu

University of Cincinnati, University College
Cincinnati, OH 45221
uc.edu

University of Toledo
Toledo, OH 43606
utoledo.edu

Ursuline College
Pepper Pike, OH 44124
ursuline.edu

Oklahoma

East Central University
Ada, OK 74820
ecok.edu

Rose State College
Oklahoma City, OK 73110
rose.edu

Tulsa Community College
Tulsa, OK 74119
tulsacc.edu

University of Oklahoma Law Center
Norman, OK 73019
ou.edu

University of Tulsa
Tulsa, OK 74104
utulsa.edu

Oregon

Pioneer Pacific College
Wilsonville, OR 97070
pioneerpacificcollege.com

Pennsylvania

Berks Technical Institute
Reading, PA 19610
berkstech.com

Bucks County Community College
Newtown, PA 18940
bucks.edu

Cedar Crest College
Allentown, PA 18104
cedarcrest.edu

Central Pennsylvania College
Summerdale, PA 17093
centralpenn.edu

Clarion University of Pennsylvania
Oil City, PA 16301
clarion.edu

Community College of Philadelphia
Philadelphia, PA 19130
ccp.cc.pa.us

Delaware County Community College
Media, PA 19063
dccc.edu

Duquesne University
Pittsburgh, PA 15282
duq.edu

Gannon University
Erie, PA 16541
gannon.edu

Harrisburg Area Community College
Harrisburg, PA 17110
hacc.edu

Lehigh Carbon Community College
Schnecksville, PA 18078
lccc.edu

Marywood University
Scranton, PA 18509
marywood.edu

Northampton Community College
Bethlehem, PA 18020
northampton.edu

Peirce College
Philadelphia, PA 19102
peirce.edu

Pennsylvania College of Technology
Williamsport, PA 17701
pct.edu

Villanova University
Villanova, PA 19085
villanova.edu

Rhode Island

Johnson & Wales University
Providence, RI 02903
jwu.edu

Roger Williams University
Bristol, RI 02809
rwu.edu

South Carolina

Aiken Technical College
Aiken, SC 29802
aik.tec.sc.us

Central Carolina Technical College
Sumter, SC 29150
cctech.edu

Florence-Darlington Technical College
Florence, SC 29501
flo.tec.sc.us

Greenville Technical College
Greenville, SC 29607
gvltec.edu

Horry-Georgetown Technical College
Myrtle Beach, SC 29577
hor.tec.sc.us

Midlands Technical College
Columbia, SC 29202
midlandstech.com

Technical College of the Lowcountry
Beaufort, SC 29901
tcl.tec.sc.us

Trident Technical College
Charleston, SC 29403
tridenttech.edu

South Dakota

National American University
Rapid City, SD 57709-1780
national.edu

Western Dakota Technical Institute
Rapid City, SD 57703
westerndakotatech.org

Tennessee

Chattanooga State Technical Community College
Chattanooga, TN 37421
chattanoogastate.edu

Cleveland State Community College
Cleveland, TN 37320
clscc.cc.tn.us

Draughons Junior College
Clarksville, TN 37040
draughons.org

Draughons Junior College
Nashville, TN 37217
draughons.org

Pellissippi State Technical Community College
Knoxville, TN 37933
pstcc.edu

Roane State Community College
Harriman, TN 37748
rscc.cc.tn.us

South College
Knoxville, TN 37917
southcollegetn.edu

Southwest Tennessee Community College
Memphis, TN 38134-7693
stcc.cc.tn.us

University of Memphis
Memphis, TN 38152
memphis.edu

University of Tennessee, Chattanooga
Chattanooga, TN 37403
utc.edu

Volunteer State Community College
Gallatin, TN 37066
vscc.cc.tn.us

Walters State Community College
Morristown, TN 37813
wscc.cc.tn.us

Texas

Blinn College
Bryan, TX 77805
blinn.edu

Central Texas College
Killeen, TX 76540
ctcd.cc.tx.us

Del Mar College
Corpus Christi, TX 78404
davlin.net

El Centro College
Dallas, TX 75202
dcccd.edu

Lamar State College, Port Arthur
Port Arthur, TX 77641
lamarpa.edu

Lee College
Baytown, TX 77522
lee.edu

McLennan Community College
Waco, TX 76708
mclennan.edu

Midland College
Midland, TX 79705
midland.edu

North Harris College
Houston, TX 77073
nhmccd.edu

San Antonio College
San Antonio, TX 78212
accd.edu

San Jacinto College, North
Houston, TX 77062
sjcd.edu

South Texas Community College
McAllen, TX 78501
stcc.cc.us

Stephen F. Austin State University
Nacogdoches, TX 75962
sfasu.edu

Tarrant County College
Hurst, TX 76054
tccd.net

Texas A&M University at Commerce
Commerce, TX 75429
tamu-commerce.edu

Texas State University, San Marcos
San Marcos, TX 78666
txstate.edu

Texas Woman's University
Denton, TX 76204
twu.edu

Utah

Mountain West College
West Valley City, UT 84119
cci.edu

Utah Valley State College
Orem, UT 84058
uvsc.edu

Vermont

Woodbury College
Montpelier, VT 05602
woodbury-college.edu

Virginia

J. Sargeant Reynolds Community College
Richmond, VA 23285
jsr.cc.va.us

Marymount University
Arlington, VA 22207
marymount.edu

National College of Business and Technology
Salem, VA 24153
educorp.edu

Virginia Center for Paralegal Studies
Fredericksburg, VA 22405
virginiaparalegalstudies.com

Washington

Edmonds Community College
Lynnwood, WA 98036
edcc.edu

Highline Community College
Des Moines, WA 98198
highline.edu

Pierce College
Lakewood, WA 98498
pierce.ctc.edu

Skagit Valley College
Mount Vernon, WA 98273
skagit.ctc.edu

South Puget Sound Community College
Olympia, WA 98512
spscc.ctc.edu

Spokane Community College
Spokane, WA 99217
scc.spokane.edu

Tacoma Community College
Tacoma, WA 98466
tacoma.ctc.edu

West Virginia

Marshall Community & Technical College
Huntington, WV 25755
marshall.edu

Wisconsin

Chippewa Valley Technical College
Eau Claire, WI 54701
chippewa.tec.wi.us

Lakeshore Technical College
Cleveland, WI 53015
gotoltc.edu

Milwaukee Area Technical College
Milwaukee, WI 53233
matc.edu

Northeast Wisconsin Technical College
Green Bay, WI 54307
nwtc.edu

Western Wisconsin Technical College
La Crosse, WI 54601
wwtc.edu

Wyoming

Casper College
Casper, WY 82601
caspercollege.edu

Laramie County Community College
Cheyenne, WY 82007
lccc.cc.wy.us

Recommended Reading

The books listed here should give you a good overview of the paralegal profession and answer most of any questions you have. Your library or an online search might also yield titles of interest.

Paralegal Books

Bogen, Deborah. *Paralegal Success: Going from Good to Great in the New Century*. Pearson Education, 1999.

Cannon, Therese A. *Ethics and Professional Responsibility for Paralegals*. Aspen Publishers, 2003.

Cefrey, Holly. *Choosing a Career as a Paralegal*. Rosen Publishing Group, 2001.

Cheeseman, Henry, and Thomas F. Goldman. *Paralegal Professional: Essentials*. Prentice Hall, 2003.

———. *The Paralegal Professional*. Pearson Education, 2002.

Cinocca, Tracy. *Careers in the Law: Success without College*. Barron's Educational, 2001.

Davis, Mary Lee. *Working in Law and Justice.* Lerner Publishing Group, 1999.

Edwards, Linda, and J. Stanley Edwards. *Introduction to Paralegal Studies and the Law: A Practical Approach.* Delmar Learning, 2001.

Estrin, Chere B. *Paralegal Career Guide.* Prentice Hall, 2001.

———. *Successful Paralegal Job Search Guide.* Delmar Learning, 2001.

Hull, Terry, and Vicki Brittain. *Paralegal Handbook.* Delmar Learning, 2001.

Jordan, Paul. *Paralegal Studies: An Introduction.* Delmar Learning, 2001.

Justice Research Association. *Your Criminal Justice Career: A Guidebook.* Prentice Hall, 2002.

The Lawyer's Almanac 2004: The Leading Reference to Vital Facts and Figures about the Legal Profession. Aspen Publishing, 2004.

McKinney, Anne. *Real Résumés for Legal and Paralegal Jobs.* Prep Publishing, 2004.

Quinlan, Kathryn A. *Paralegal.* Capstone Press, 1998.

Schneeman, Angela. *Paralegal Careers.* Delmar Learning, 2000.

Southard, Jo Lynn. *Paralegal Career Starter.* LearningExpress, 2002.

Statsky, William P. *Introduction to Paralegalism: Perspectives, Problems, and Skills.* Delmar Learning, 2002.

Wagner, Andrea. *How to Land Your First Paralegal Job: An Insider's Guide to the Fastest Growing Profession of the New Millennium.* Pearson Education, 2000.

Warner, Ralph E., Catherine Elias-Jermany, and Stephen Elias. *Independent Paralegal's Handbook.* Nolo, 2004.

General Job Search and Career Books

Adams, Bob, and Laura Morin. *The Complete Résumé & Job Search Book for College Students*. Adams Media Corporation, 1999.

Bloch, Deborah Perlmutter. *How to Get Your First Job and Keep It*. McGraw-Hill, 2002.

Bolles, Richard Nelson. *What Color Is Your Parachute 2004: A Practical Manual for Job-Hunters and Career Changers*. Ten Speed Press, 2003.

Cunningham, John R. *The Inside Scoop: Recruiters Share Their Tips on Job Search Success with College Students*. McGraw-Hill, 2001.

Deluca, Matthew J. *Best Answers to the 201 Most Frequently Asked Interview Questions*. McGraw-Hill, 1996.

Deluca, Matthew, and Nanette Deluca. *More Best Answers to the 201 Most Frequently Asked Interview Questions*. McGraw-Hill, 2001.

Drake, John D. *The Perfect Interview: How to Get the Job You Really Want*. Fine Publications, 2002.

Eisenberg, Ronni. *Organize Your Job Search!* Hyperion Press, 2000.

Gale, Linda, and Barry Gale. *Discover What You're Best At: A Complete Career System That Lets You Test Yourself to Discover Your Own True Career Abilities*. Simon and Schuster, 1998.

Garber, Janet. *Getting a Job*. Silver Lining Books, 2003.

Graber, Steven, and Barry Littmann. *Everything Online Job Search Book: Find the Jobs, Send Your Résumé, and Land the Career of Your Dreams—All Online!* Adams Media Corporation, 2000.

Greene, Susan D., and Melanie C. Martel. *The Ultimate Job Hunter's Guidebook*. Houghton Mifflin Company, 2000.

Griffiths, Bob. *Do What You Love for the Rest of Your Life: A Practical Guide to Career Change and Personal Renewal.* Random House, 2001.

Jansen, Julie. *I Don't Know What I Want, but I Know It's Not This: A Step-by-Step Guide to Finding Gratifying Work.* Penguin USA, 2003.

McKinney, Anne, ed. *Real Résumés for Career Changers: Actual Résumés and Cover Letters.* PREP Publishing, 2000.

O'Neill, Lucy. *Job Smarts.* Scholastic Library Publishing, 2001.

Résumés for First-Time Job Hunters. McGraw-Hill, 2005.

Shar, Barbara, and Barbara Smith. *I Could Do Anything if I Only Knew What It Was: How to Discover What You Really Want and How to Get It.* Dell Publishing, 1995.

Tieger, Paul, and Barbara Barron-Tieger. *Do What You Are: Discover the Perfect Career for You through the Secrets of Personality Type.* Little, Brown and Company, 2001.

Whitcomb, Susan Britton, and Pat Kendall. *e-Resumes: Everything You Need to Know about Using Electronic Résumés to Tap into Today's Hot Job Market.* McGraw-Hill, 2001.

About the Author

Alice Fins has worked in a variety of paralegal-type jobs, although she has never actually held the title of paralegal. After six years of high school and college teaching, she combined two personal interests—law and writing—by entering the field of legal publishing. During her time as editor of *Consumerism*, a weekly newsletter published by Commerce Clearing House, she became acquainted with many lawyers and nonlawyers writing on various aspects of the law.

With a move to the nation's capital came a new position writing and editing *Guidepost*, the newspaper of the American Association for Counseling and Development. In this job she covered hearings on Capitol Hill and represented the association before government leaders and other associations. Much of her background in legal research and procedure came into play in these activities.

After she accepted the position of director of information for the American Bar Association's Governmental Relations Office, she wrote a monthly newsletter describing legislation of interest to the organized bar and supervised the writing of other legislative documents. She also answered inquiries about lawyers and paralegals.

Her experiences in this position gave her an acquaintance with a great many paralegals working in government.

Since she left the ABA, Ms. Fins has written a number of books, including several for McGraw-Hill. These include *Women in Science*, *Women in Engineering*, and *Women in Communications*.

She also has served as a consultant on publications for a variety of organizations, including:

- The Equity Institute, Bethesda, Maryland
- National Education Association, Washington, D.C.
- Council for the Advancement of Standards for Student Services/Development Programs, Washington, D.C.
- National Commission of Unemployment Compensation
- President's Commission for the Study of Ethical Problems in Medicine and Biomedical and Behavioral Research
- Reproductive Toxicology Center, Washington, D.C.
- Worldwatch Institute, Washington, D.C.
- American Federation of Information Processing Societies, Arlington, Virginia
- National School Boards Association, Washington, D.C.

Ms. Fins is the author of major articles in the ERIC Clearinghouse on Higher Education and in the National Clearinghouse on School Violence and Vandalism Prevention. She is widely published in educational and career publications. She is listed in *Contemporary Authors*, *Who's Who of American Women*, *Washington Media Women*, and the *Washington Independent Writers' Directory*.

This edition was revised and updated by Mark Rowh, author of a number of books on careers published by McGraw-Hill.